HOW TO PUBLISH
YOUR POETRY

HELENE CIARAVINO

SQUAREONE
WRITERS GUIDES

Cover Designer: Phaedra Mastrocola
In-House Editor: Karen J. Hay
Typesetter: Gary A. Rosenberg

Square One Publishers
Garden City Park, NY 11040
(516) 535-2010
www.squareonepublishers.com

Publisher's Cataloging-in-Publication Data
Ciaravino, Helene.
    How to publish your poetry : a complete guide to finding the right
publishers for your work / by Helene Ciaravino.
        p. cm. — (A Square One writer's guide)
        Includes bibliographical references and index.
        ISBN 0-7570-0001-0

        1. Poetry—Marketing. I. Title. II. Series.

    PN1059.M3 C53 2000   070.5'2—dc21
                                                 00-010009

Printed in the United States of America

10   9   8   7   6   5   4   3   2

CONTENTS

For all the poet souls
who have the courage
and the conviction
to become bards.

ACKNOWLEDGMENTS

With greatest sincerity, I thank the following people:

My publisher and friend, Rudy Shur, for giving me the opportunity and much of the knowledge and experience necessary to write this guide.

My editor and friend, Karen Hay, for the unconditional support and guidance, as well as the polishing and piecing together of material.

The many people who, in voice and in text, provided information for my manuscript, and all those at Square One Publishers who then turned my manuscript into a book.

My dear family and friends, who have always respected my drive to write and who have always nurtured my poet's heart.

A Note on Gender Usage

To avoid long and awkward phrasing within sentences, the publisher has chosen to alternate the use of male and female pronouns according to chapter. Therefore, when referring to the third-person writer or editor, odd-numbered chapters use male pronouns, while even-numbered chapters employ female pronouns, to give acknowledgment to writers and editors of both genders. Please realize that no offense or slight is intended.

$\mathcal{I}$NTRODUCTION

There is a quiet holiness associated with a poet such as Emily Dickinson. She never committed to the struggle for publication in her lifetime. In fact, in a letter to a literary critic who became a long-term correspondent, Dickinson wrote: "I smile when you suggest that I delay 'to publish'—that being foreign to my thought as Firmament to Fin. . . . My Barefoot Rank is better." Most of Dickinson's original poetry was not found until after her death. Whether the poet believed the literary world was simply not ready for her, or whether she truly had no desire to see her verses go public, is a subject that allows only speculation. But we do know that as she got older, Dickinson became increasingly offended by publication and fame. She died an unfamiliar name, an unpublished poet. Something tells us that Dickinson would have it no other way. Posthumous praise allowed a beautiful ending to the story of the poet who dressed solely in white and secluded herself within her parents' Amherst house.

But let's face it. You don't always dress in white. (In fact, if you're amongst the poets in Manhattan, there's a chance you

From the Poet's Pen

Emily Dickinson expressed distaste for the publication process, writing:

Publication is the auction of the mind of man.

Yet many poets feel their work is not complete until it is shared through print publication, and certainly don't find publication to be, as Dickinson wrote, "so foul a thing."

dress only in black.) You're not hiding in your childhood bedroom. And, considering that you picked up this book, you probably won't be content until you see your work in print. Your poetry means a lot to you—it is hours of red-hot emotions, exhausting expression, and painstaking editing—and you are willing to fight for publication. It takes energy and time to make it into a magazine or literary journal, and perhaps someday, to publish a collection of your own. You need a little guidance and a couple of ideas. Well, this is the book for you.

How to Publish Your Poetry offers practical information on how to break into the world of print poetry. The information is gathered from extensive, current literature on, and advice from, the publishing world. It also stems from the experience I gained in my years as an editor, and from my passions as a poet who has been writing and studying verse for over a decade. I understand and support not only your love of the poetry craft, but also your desire to share it with others. Your journey is my journey, and everything that I suggest is based in the realm of reasonable endeavors. You've probably dreamed about being in print for a long time, but perhaps you are intimidated by the unfamiliar field of publishing or simply don't know where to begin. Here's the good news: if you read the information and follow the organized strategy in this book, you'll *greatly* increase your odds of getting published. You've had the passion for a long time; now you have the system.

Chapter 1 introduces you to the whole process of "getting into print" by guiding you into the proper mindset. The Square One System will work most effectively if you have a realistic view of poetry publication and if you establish short-term goals. Chapter 2 reveals the basics of the publishing industry, including what kinds of publishers are available to poets and what types of publications you should target. Chapter 3 suggests great market resources for locating publications, and also highlights the importance of finding your best audience. Chapters 4 and 5 get to the nitty-gritty, discussing what to include in your submission packages and then the system behind sending them out. Chapter 6 covers what to do with the results. It also offers some other options in case things don't work out the way you planned.

There is one thing, in particular, that this guidebook is designed *not* to do: overwhelm you. All of the information is broken down into clearly labeled sections; the advice is realistic; and the steps of the system are well-paced. *How to Publish Your Poetry* provides a great working knowledge of the publication process. So let's start you on your way to becoming what you've dreamt of for a long time—a published poet.

From the Poet's Pen

All hail, sweet poet, more full of more strong fire, Than hath or shall enkindle any spirit. . .

From the poem "To Mr. T.W." by John Donne

CHAPTER 1

$\mathcal{U}$NDERSTANDING YOUR GOALS

Putting yourself in the proper mindset is the first thing to do at the start of any journey, be it professional, intellectual, physical, or spiritual. The journey toward the publication of your poetry is no exception. Ask yourself, "What are my goals, and what's it going to take to reach them?" By clearly understanding your goals, you will accomplish a more efficient, more successful journey.

"Winging it" may be dramatic, romantic, and even randomly successful. However, for the majority of the poets who seek publication, serious preparation for what's ahead is more productive. That means developing a strong sense of commitment. It means using what used to be your "free time" to the fullest. The best preparation for the process includes four things: cultivating a realistic viewpoint concerning being a published poet; setting a short-term finish line in order to motivate yourself; clearing time and space for what it's going to take; and selecting the best poems for submission. If you accomplish these, then you will be in great shape to tackle the Square One System for getting your work into print.

BEING REALISTIC ABOUT BEING A POET

In ancient Celtic culture, poets were revered as great teachers and historians. They did not own their own houses or grow their own food. Instead, they traveled the countryside, receiving lodging and meals in exchange for the entertainment and knowledge they supplied. Similarly, in the Europe of the Dark Ages, traveling madrigals entranced audiences with their lyrical poetry. They were troubadours, making a full living off their music and verses. Later, in Medieval Italy, respected poets were funded by wealthy patrons. These patrons "wore" their poets like status-symbol accessories. But let's face it: in today's world, the poet cannot make a living on poetry alone.

Despite the efforts of many literary magazines and arts organizations, modern culture does not tangibly reward the poet. Our modern world feeds such fields as finance, law, professional sports, and computer technology—not poetry. So as the old saying goes, "keep your day job." The publication of poetry is not lucrative or stable enough to rely on as a career. Keep doing what you're doing to put dinner on the table and paper in your printer; maintain perspective. In this chapter, we will discuss how to divvy up your time—how to continue your "normal" life and still give what it takes to publish your poetry.

A large number of respected poets happen to work within fields related to literature. Many are university professors who teach poetry and/or creative writing. Some are administrators of arts foundations and poetry centers. Quite a few are literary editors, writers for magazines, and the like. But being professionally linked to literature is certainly not a criterion for someone to write poetry, nor to publish it. Doctors, lawyers, actors, politicians, musicians, store clerks, stay-at-home parents, high-school students, and just about everyone else can find people in their positions who write poetry and share it with others in print. The important point is that 99 percent of published poets—even the most prominent of published poets—do other

It is true that a large number of recognized poets work within fields related to writing and literature. But being in a literary profession is by no means a criterion for a person to become a published and recognized poet.

things to generate or supplement their incomes. Let's look at a few examples.

James Weldon Johnson (1871–1938)

The name James Weldon Johnson strikes respect and pride in many hearts. He is considered a significant forerunner of America's Civil Rights Movement. He is also widely recognized as an American poet. Johnson had quite a number of careers, and serves as a good example for the poet who juggles many roles.

Immediately after college, Johnson became a high school principal and started writing song lyrics on the side. He composed "Lift Ev'ry Voice and Sing" in 1900, in honor of Abraham Lincoln's birthday. This song eventually became what was referred to as the "Negro National Anthem." Johnson decided to pursue his songwriting talents further, but that avenue didn't prove to be as fruitful as he had hoped, so he changed direction.

In 1906, Johnson became the U.S. Consul to Venezuela. During this significant assignment in the diplomatic corps, he published poems in *Century Magazine* and *The Independent*. A few years later, he went on to publish *The Autobiography of an Ex-Colored Man* under a pen name, which has become a crucial text in studies of Black literature and race issues. In 1920, Johnson became the organizer for the National Association for the Advancement of Colored People (NAACP). Over the following years, he would continue his literary career, editing *The Book of American Negro Poetry* in 1922, and publishing his own book of poetry titled *God's Trombones* in 1927.

James Weldon Johnson was born in 1871 in Jacksonville, Florida, and attended Atlanta University. In 1900, on the occasion of Lincoln's Birthday, Johnson wrote the song "Lift Ev'ry Voice and Sing," which became known as the "Negro National Anthem." In 1920, he became the national organizer for the National Association for the Advancement of Colored People (NAACP). Two years later, he edited *The Book of American Negro Poetry*, a major contribution to the history of African-American literature. Johnson died in 1938.

Wallace Stevens (1879–1955)

Wallace Stevens' poetry is praised by the harshest of critics—the academics. He is admired for his puzzle-like and heavily decorated verses. While his poetic voice tends to expose him as an

Wallace Stevens was born in Reading, Pennsylvania in 1879. He graduated from Harvard and went on to New York Law School. As vice president of the Hartford Accident and Indemnity Co., he composed poems on his way to and from the office. In 1914, he had four of his poems published, and began to establish an identity for himself outside the world of law and business. Though now considered one of the major American poets of the twentieth century, he did not receive widespread recognition until about a year before his death in 1955.

indulgent aesthete, the reality is that Stevens led a very normal life as a businessman who wrote poetry on the side.

During college at Harvard, Stevens' pull toward literature was already forming. He became president of the *Harvard Advocate*, in which he printed some of his poetry. Stevens started working for *The New York Herald Tribune* once he graduated, but his father (an attorney) convinced him to go to law school. Stevens practiced law for twelve years in New York, but wasn't particularly successful. So while in his late thirties, Stevens joined the staff of the Hartford Accident and Indemnity Company and was eventually promoted to its vice-presidency. He remained with that company until he died.

There's much more to the story, however. Stevens was also quietly publishing poetry in journals and small magazines during his twenties and thirties. At forty-four, he published his first book, titled *Harmonium*. Because the book was not successful, Stevens did not publish another volume for twelve years. In the meantime, he published his poems widely in literary magazines, through which he gathered himself a large audience. By the time his second, third, and succeeding volumes were published, Stevens was a sure success. Still, he kept himself removed from any swollen identity as a famous poet. In *Six American Poets: An Anthology*, editor Joel Conarroe reveals, "The recipient of various awards and honorary degrees, [Stevens] never took such accolades seriously. Returning from a Columbia University commencement in 1952, he hung up his bright new academic hood and said to his wife, 'Look, darling, I have another scalp.'"

William Carlos Williams (1883–1963)

William Carlos Williams was born in New Jersey in 1883, and began writing poetry in high school.

This great American poet started writing poetry back in high school, and decided then and there that he would succeed at two professions—medicine and poetry. Williams started making a name for himself as a poet while he was in medical school at the University of Pennsylvania. He began by publishing in small magazines, and this led him to set a life-long literary goal: to create a new and distinctively American voice in poetry.

While at medical school, Williams had the fortunate experience of becoming friends with the infamous Ezra Pound. Expatriot Pound, favoring the British publishing industry to that of his native land's, used his influence to have Williams' first poetry collection (*The Tempers*) published in London. The rest is literary history. Williams' well-known works, such as *In the American Grain* and *Paterson,* accomplish what the poet set out to do. Although Williams developed an impressive literary career, he also continued a medical practice in obstetrics and gynecology throughout his life. In fact, his role as a doctor exposed Williams to many personalities and experiences that enriched his poetry.

Williams went on to receive a medical degree from the University of Pennsylvania, where he befriended writer Ezra Pound, who arranged for the London publication of Williams' collection, *The Tempers.* Returning to Rutherford, Williams embarked on a prolific career as a poet, novelist, essayist, and playwright. Williams continued writing until his death in 1963.

T. S. Eliot (1888–1965)

This poet, whose full name is Thomas Stearns Eliot, has influenced history with his work. Some scholars and critics argue that Eliot's "The Waste Land" is the most significant literary piece of the twentieth century. Eliot seems to embody all that the term "poet" implies. So you may be rather surprised to learn that he was not a full-time poet. T.S. Eliot held regular paying jobs, just like you and me. Over the years of his life, this Nobel Prize winner was a teacher, an editor, and even an employee of Lloyd's Bank.

Writer Ezra Pound is responsible for discovering Eliot's promise as a poet. Pound used his influence to have Eliot published in the respected journal *Poetry* in 1915. Eliot's first poetry book, titled *Prufrock and Other Observations,* was published two years later. His literary career took off from there. Yet even when his reputation skyrocketed, Eliot maintained a career outside poetry. He served as editor of *Criterion,* a literary journal, and then became a director and literary editor for Faber & Faber, a distinguished publishing house.

Thomas Stearns Eliot was born in Missouri in 1888, and graduated from Harvard University. In 1914, Eliot moved to England, and there he met Ezra Pound, who assisted in the publication of his work in a number of magazines. By 1930, he was the most dominant figure in poetry and literary criticism in the English-speaking world. He became both a publisher and playwright, and received the Nobel Prize for Literature. Eliot died in London in 1965.

Carolyn Kizer (1925–)

Carolyn Kizer was born in Spokane, Washington in 1925, and graduated from Sarah Lawrence College in 1945. In 1959, she founded *Poetry Northwest*, and served as its editor until 1965. Kizer was also poet-in-residence at the University of North Carolina and Ohio University, and Chancellor of The Academy of American Poets. She has received numerous awards for her poetry, and is the author of seven poetry books.

Carolyn Kizer is considered a significant American poet. She has published seven books of poetry, including *Yin* (1984), which won the Pulitzer Prize. In addition to her poetry books, Kizer has written several books on the craft of prose and poetry, and has done numerous translations. Furthermore, Kizer is an active editor. For example, she edited *100 Great Poems by Women* (1995) and *The Essential Clare* (1992).

Previously, Kizer founded *Poetry Northwest*, a very respected literary journal. She served as editor of the publication from its start in 1959 until 1965. Over the following five years, she was the first Director of the Literature Program, a branch of the National Endowment for the Arts. She has received numerous awards, and is also a Chancellor of the Academy of American Poets. From her long list of achievements, it is easy to see that Kizer has always maintained an active career life outside of her poetry.

John Updike (1932–)

John Updike was born in Shillington, Pennsylvania in 1932, and was educated at Harvard University. From 1955 to 1957, Updike was a staff writer for *The New Yorker* magazine. Among his best-known works are his novels about the life and times of character Harry "Rabbit" Angstrom. Updike has won the National Book Award, and has twice been awarded the Pulitzer Prize.

John Updike is known for his best-selling novels. His "Rabbit" series (named for Harry Rabbit, a character in the books) has entertained countless readers. Updike has collected numerous awards for these books, including two Pulitzer Prizes for Fiction, three American National Book Awards, and the National Book Critics' Circle Award. Yet he does a lot more than write novels. Updike is an essayist, a critic, and even a skilled and published poet!

Updike's poetry is actually what instigated his professional writing career. Back in the 1950s, Updike submitted a poem to *The New Yorker* and it was accepted. Thus began a long relationship with the magazine and with the publishing world. In fact, Updike's first published book was a collection of poetry titled *The Carpentered Hen and Other Tame Creatures* (1958). While novels are his big business, Updike has published quite a few poetry collections as well.

Luci Tapahonso (1953–)

Luci Tapahonso is one of America's more recent successful poets. Loyal to her Navajo roots in New Mexico, Tapahonso crafts her poetry around her ethnic history and experiences. This prolific poet publishes in commercial magazines, academic journals, poetry journals, and anthologies. She has also published quite a few poetry/prose books and a children's book. Her collections, such as *Horses Rush In* and *Sáanii Dahataał/The Women Are Singing: Poems and Stories,* are read everywhere from universities to kitchen tables.

But in addition to being a poet, Tapahonso is a university professor. She is presently an Associate Professor of English at the University of Kansas, Lawrence, where she teaches Poetry Writing and American Indian Literature. As if that didn't fill her time, Tapahonso is on the editorial board of *wicazo sa review,* and has been active on other editorial boards in the past. She has served as a juror for the Poetry Society of America, the Association Writing Program Award, and the Stan Steiner Writing Awards. Furthermore, Tapahonso holds positions on several prestigious writing and arts boards, too numerous to mention here. She has done extensive anthology editing and contributing, as well. To top it all off, Tapahonso has five children!

Luci Tapahonso was born in Shiprock, New Mexico in 1953. Navajo was her first language, but she learned English at boarding school, and began writing poetry when she was only nine years old. Although she has been teaching English on the university level since her college graduation, Tapahonso's poetry has always deeply reflected her Navajo roots. She is a recipient of the Frost Place Poet-in-Residence award.

ESTABLISHING YOUR GOALS

You have survived the reality check and are still heading toward the publication process. After all, you never composed your poetry in hopes of monetary gain; you wrote for some other reason. You had a goal in mind, be it personal catharsis or social change. That brings us to our next step.

Why do you write poetry? Why do you want to publish?

Even the Poet Laureate...

Even Robert Pinsky, three-time United States Poet Laureate, is not a full-time poet. Among his many roles, Pinsky is a professor and an editor. He publishes many critical essays, and donates a great amount of time to the development and implementation of programs that increase the awareness and reading of poetry. That sure puts things in perspective!

Pinsky reminds us that the motivation to write poetry, and to stick to the process, best stems from a sincere sense of responsibility to answer some of the world's questions. According to Pinsky, having an audience is much less important than having an inescapable calling to respond, through writing, to the situations around you. In *Poetry and the World,* Pinsky remarks, "The response may be a contradiction, it may be unwanted, it may go unheeded, it may be embraced but twisted . . . but it is owed, and the sense that it is owed is a basic requirement for the poet's good feeling about the art." From this, we learn that a healthy attitude toward writing poetry does not come from how many hours can be spent on it per day, or how many books we have published, but from the strength of the call we feel inside to carry the art of writing poetry to fruition. So don't feel like any less of a poet if you have to work nine-to-five and raise three children while you maintain your poetry life on the side. The fact that you feel the call and are responding to it means that you already are a true poet, regardless of where those stanzas end up.

Helpful Hint

Setting a short-term goal —an accessible finish line— will help you to maintain a healthy motivation.

Once you've examined your motivations enough to answer these questions, you will be better able to establish your goals. It's okay to say, "I want to see my own book of poetry on the shelf someday." We all need dreams, and some of us attain them. But it is also important to have a clear understanding of your immediate, short-term goals. By designing a reasonable plan, you are less likely to become discouraged and overwhelmed.

Why Do You Write Poetry?

One thing that all poets have in common is the drive for creative expression—desiring to use more than conventional, standard discourse to carry out a discussion. Poetry can involve rhythm, sound, association, and imagery. Through it, the unlike can become like and, for a brief moment, the universe has a shot at making sense. But the motivations behind the use of poetry vary from poet to poet, and even from poem to poem. Let's consider some of these motivations.

Some poets write mainly for therapeutic healing. A healing process takes place as the poet articulates his anxieties on paper. Pieces of the puzzle are laid out, perhaps enabling the writer to start putting a picture together. If a poet writes predominantly for therapeutic reasons, he should be extra critical when judging whether his poetry is publishable or not. In his agenda to "write out loud" and affect release, he may not have fully developed form, line breaks, rhythm, pauses, imagery, etc. The craft of the work was probably less of a priority than emotional satisfaction. Plus, the thoughts behind the poems are vivid and alive for *him*, but what comes out on paper may not be universal enough or clear enough for a larger readership. Of course, on the other hand, the poems may be fine specimens of art and very capable of helping others to release emotions. But this type of poet should seriously consider the possibility that, if the poems were developed for very private gain, they should remain within a private space.

Motivations behind the use of poetry vary from poet to poet, and even from poem to poem.

Quite differently, some poets write with an audience in mind from the very beginning. They write to entertain, to discuss social values, to emotionally move the reader, etc. These writers are more concerned with the public role of poetry, and are more likely to watch the artistic details. After all, they must keep in mind that editors and critics will be looking at the particulars. Publication is a natural step for these poets, but only when their craft has sufficiently matured.

Finally, some poets are motivated by the desire to achieve membership among an exciting group of people. There is a sense of community, intelligence, and imagination among poets. Writing poetry automatically places the writer in a "club" of sorts. The identity found in being a poet is attractive and, somehow, demands respect. Perhaps this is left over from the days when poets were regarded as the gifted ones—the storytellers, responsible for passing on culture, history, and myth. We shouldn't lose this respect for poets. But in order to be truly successful at poetry and its publication, a writer's motivations must be more than cosmetic. Ultimately, the fascination should be with the craft and its effects, not with acceptance into an alternative, trendy crowd.

Think about why *you* write poetry. It will help you to decide whether or not you are actually prepared for the publication process. No matter what, realize that writing good poetry is not an easy task. It involves a lot of work, even if you have natural talent and a good ear. If you think you have the skill and a healthy motivation, move ahead.

Why Do You Want To Publish?

You've studied your reasons for sitting down and writing poetry. Now, why do you want to send it out into the rough hands of the public? More than anything else, this question involves expectation. If you want to publish your poetry, you have expectations about what its publication is going to do for you and your readers.

As we discussed under "Being Realistic About Being a Poet," you are not going to receive monetary payment at the beginning of your poetry career. And even if you become a renowned poet, the position is not particularly lucrative. So your reasons to publish should not be linked to financial gain. Perhaps you want to publish because you have a true and sincere desire to share. Maybe it is only through publication that you can fully realize your dream and feel satisfied. If this sounds familiar, your heart is in the right place. You have the spark necessary to keep at the publication process until you see your work in print.

Maybe you want to publish as a way to advance your full-time career. Many professors who are pursuing tenure-track

From the Poet's Pen

In his poem titled "Digging," Seamus Heaney views his writer's pen as a powerful tool akin to the spade that his father and grandfather used to work the fields:

Between my finger
and my thumb
The squat pen rests.
I'll dig with it.

Why do you dig with your pen? Why do you want to be published?

positions must accomplish annual publishing. Also, teachers who simply want to swell their resumes may benefit from being published in journals and magazines. The same goes for editors and those who seek positions on arts boards and in community programs. Having a list of publication credits means that you have been accepted—by at least several editors and audiences—as a gifted writer, and that your voice is reaching people outside your own four walls. In this situation, again, you have strong motivation that will serve you well, but the motivation is more professional than artistic.

There is, of course, that strong desire to leave a mark on the world and somehow find immortality through your efforts. Every poet probably has a touch of this. Yet not too much fame is available in the poetry world. If you are among those who reach large-scale recognition, you will be an exception. For now, concentrate on reasonable reasons to publish—most appropriately, because you have a talent from which you think others can benefit, and because you'd enjoy the satisfaction of unleashing your poetic voice. If you seek publication out of sheer desire for attention, you'll be working at a disadvantage. As soon as rejection slips start pouring in, your self-esteem will be shaken. You might turn completely away from poetry as an art and away from publishing as an industry.

Finally, for every writer, getting published signifies worthiness. Most of us are social creatures and we like to win the approval and love of our neighbors. So seeing your own work in print can make you feel like you've done something right, something good. But how big are your notions of getting into print? What is "success" to you?

How Far Off Are Your Goals?

In preparing to start out on your publication journey, it is crucial that you isolate realistic and short-term goals. Every poet who seeks print publication dreams about being read and admired

The poet who seeks publication primarily for attention is working at a disadvantage; rejection slips will shake his self-esteem, and he is likely to turn away from poetry. Those who have cultivated a higher purpose are the poets who have what it takes to be successful at the publication process.

three hundred years from now. Every such poet desires to be a voice that will change many. But if you rely on long-range vision and the highest of hopes, you are bound to miss the wonderful pleasures and possibilities that are right in front of you. In addition, you are bound to feel so angered and dejected by the publication process that you will eventually give up. And in this process, persistence is key. Here's some simple advice: keep your dreams, but meet your goals. Realistic and short-term goals will allow you to maintain your passion and motivation.

If you are truly interested in poetry as a literary genre—in its rules and its changes, in its ability to foster a national identity and cultural awareness, in its almost scientific patterns of form, syntax, meter, etc.—then you want to gear yourself toward the academic and literary magazines in the short term. You are interested in poetry as a fine art, as these publications are. The nice part about being motivated by true passion for poetry is that you will find satisfaction in being published in any magazine that you, yourself, respect. Aim toward getting individual poems accepted into print. This is a very manageable short-term goal. In the long run, you may look toward accumulating enough publication credits to consider a collection. However, this latter goal should not be the focus at the present time. Legitimate small presses, and certainly larger publishing houses, will rarely invest in an author who has no credits to his name. You need to build your reputation slowly.

Similarly, if you have professional reasons to publish, aim toward academic and literary publications, especially ones that have national or large-scale circulations. You'll want to publish with serious, respected magazines. You probably have developed your work enough to make your way into recognized publications within a year or so. In the long run, if you are successful at publishing individual poems, a collection might be possible. But again, focus on getting individual poems into print.

If you decided that you write for sheer fun and entertainment—if you like jingles, lyrical rhymes, comedic puns, and

Helpful Hint

A poet builds his reputation slowly. Shoot for getting individual poems published at the start of your career, instead of an entire collection.

tongue twisters—your short-term goal should be to publish poems in a couple of light-hearted niche magazines, *not* journals and quarterlies. Community newsletters also offer possible markets, as they often seek local and colorful voices. In addition, seriously consider researching the greeting card industry and contests for theme poetry. Chapter 6 offers more information on both of these options. A long-term goal might be to work your way up to a few acceptances in commercial (possibly children's) magazines that accept poetry around the holidays, in theme issues, etc. However, breaking into the commercial market is certainly not easy, nor is it common.

It is important to define "short-term" in the poetry publication process. Keep in mind that it often takes editors several months to respond to submission packages, and then, most of the responses are rejections. So when you set a short-term goal of publishing several individual poems, give yourself approximately one to two years if you take an aggressive approach, three years if you have less time to pursue publication. Building your publication credits takes quite a while, not to mention considerable patience and persistence.

Chapter 2 further discusses the options that poets have in the publishing industry. It explores the available but often disadvantageous opportunities such as publishing a full book through a vanity press, and submitting your poems to big magazines that rarely publish new poets. The importance of establishing reasonable short-term goals will become even more clear.

In the world of poetry publication, "short-term goals" refer to goals that are reasonably attained within one to three years.

MAKING TIME AND SPACE

You've cleared your mind of the clutter, putting motivation into proper perspective and organizing your goals. Now it's time to clear a place in your schedule and in your home, so that you can tend to this publication process. If you have a "nine-to-five" job and/or a family to raise, scheduling poetry time and organizing poetry space may not be too easy. But this section contains pointers that will certainly help you out.

The Time Slots

In our fast-paced culture, we shove a lot into the twenty-four hour day. Now you're going to add a whole new agenda to your "things to do" list. Working toward publication involves a good deal of research and a good deal of upkeep. Let's do a quick tour of the publication process—a basic outline of what the Square One System for publishing poetry is going to involve—and then we'll talk about how to organize your time.

Your journey into print can be quite smooth and easy if you follow the steps in this book. First, read through the book once. It won't take you long. Split it up over a couple of sessions; keep the book by your bed for nighttime reading, and beside your morning coffee for a few AM pages. The preview will give you an idea of the entire process. Then settle down for action.

You'll need to spend some time figuring out what kind of people you are going to market your poetry toward: academics; conservatives; spiritualists; adults only; nature lovers; etc. Once you choose your avenues, the most time-consuming part begins. You have to spend a good deal of time checking out your markets and deciding on which specific publications to target. That involves making trips to the library and the book-stores to consult resource texts and magazines, and time on the Internet (if you choose) doing additional searches. Depending on how much time you can give per week, this could take, for example, one to two weeks or one to two months. Then the more in-depth research begins. You must contact each selected publication for submission guidelines, and look at each publication (when possible) for a better understanding of its audience. And you want to do this at a healthy pace—try not to rush yourself, and definitely don't do it halfway, because that always creates stress.

Then comes the point at which you start putting together your submission packages. There's a lot to do, including the composition of cover letters, the cosmetic preparation of your poem print-outs, the labeling and stamping of return envelopes, the packing and the mailing. You may even concern yourself with formally copyrighting your work (although it's not a *must*). This will add extra steps to the process.

When the eight-week waiting period comes around the corner, you may be tempted to consider your "poetry time slots" vacant. Yet, there's always more research to do—for the next battery of mail-outs. And don't forget to keep up with your writing in the meantime. All this means that you need to reserve a decent amount of space during each month for your poetry goals.

First, try to commit to "poetry business" for at least a few hours every week. You want to maintain a reasonable groove and work with the material often enough as to avoid "review sessions" that take up additional time. Also, try to slot sessions of *at least* two or three hours in length. Realize that an hour will hardly afford you time to delve deeply into your work. Longer time blocks allow for completion of thoughts, steady research, consistent editing of your cover letters and poems, etc. Your research will be less effective and your writing will suffer if you can't reach a good level of concentration.

A recent edition of *Writer's Digest* included an article by Marshall Cook titled "10 Secrets of Getting Published." One of the secrets involves the realization that you will never simply have time to write. Let's add the notion that you will never simply have time for the submission process either. Cook states, "If you want to be a published writer, you must make time for writing and marketing (and, eventually, for the book tours, of course). Use the addition/subtraction principle. If you add an hour a day writing, you must subtract an hour of something(s) else." That's certainly the truth. Don't panic—with better time management, you don't have to stop doing anything you're supposed to be doing, you just have to fit everything in more neatly.

Helpful Hint

Try to reserve *at least* two to three hours for each "poetry business" time slot. Considerable blocks of time allow for more effective research, the completion of thoughts, and better editing of your cover letters and poems.

Helpful Hint

The best poets are also readers. By continuing to read other poets' work, you will exercise your imagination, expand your writing skills, and become more familiar with poetic styles and niches.

Take a suggestion from Jeffery Zbar's article titled "20 Tips to Better Time Management," also found in *Writer's Digest*. Zbar advises that you take a few days to map your average day, writing down everything you do and at what time you do it. Learn to discriminate, asking, "Is this the best thing I can be doing at this point?" Therefore, you will become more aware of time usage. You'll also become more aware of the times that the typical "little emergencies" crop up—those little things that most people use as excuses for not doing what they're supposed to be doing. When you have a good idea of how you spend your time, start drawing up a schedule. Buy yourself a calendar: it's most efficient to have a day-by-day calendar, as well as a month spread calendar. Don't wait for the morning to make a plan for that very day. Plan your days ahead of time.

Initially, slot in the "musts," such as picking up the kids from softball practice, attending your weekly writing group meetings, etc. See what time slots remain, and begin to fill them in with the optional commitments. Zbar suggests that you note the times of the day when you are most productive. Try to work your poetry business into some of these time slots. If you leave studying markets and writing cover letters for the "11 PM to 1 AM slot" twice a week, always after a full workday, you're not likely to be very productive unless you are nocturnal.

Consider that you will need to find a time when the computer is available, the phones are relatively quiet, and a desk is free, if you share desk space. For many people who work day jobs, time for the publication process best falls into the late evening or night, before bedtime. That's okay, if you are a night person. But if you are not, dedicate a good amount of weekend time.

When waiting for responses to come in the mail, don't be anxious to fill your poetry slots with entirely different hobbies and responsibilities; consider them reserved. Use the time for reading poetry, researching additional publications, etc. Don't lose your groove. Within the next eight weeks, you should start getting responses. Then you'll want to turn to your next selection of publications and reactivate that submission process.

The Workspace

Establishing a functional workspace is essential for proper mindset. If you don't already have a home office or study area where you can work on your poetry endeavors, read this section. You will find that a well-organized, well-stocked space can make all the difference in accomplishing your goals within a reasonable amount of time.

Find a small space that you can make your own, at least for several hours per week. If you have a guestroom in your house, have it moonlight as your home office. You don't have to cover the blankets with ink stains or wallpaper the closet doors with sticky notes. Just take charge of the desk or table already there and set yourself up. Of course, not all of us have guestrooms.

Jeffery Zbar offers helpful tips for space management in a recent *Writer's Digest* "Six Keys to Home Office Success." While his article is written for freelancers who work full-time from home, the information also applies to poets who are technically running their own part-time marketing and sales strategies for poetry. Zbar makes an interesting suggestion for those of us who have *very* limited space: turn a closet into a little at-home office! There's all sorts of build-it-yourself furniture, shelving, stacking pieces, etc., that can be used to create a very compact workspace. Surely, a bedroom desk or out-of-use dining-room table works too. Just choose a space where you can keep your work, your files, and your resource texts together.

Whether an antique banker's desk, an IKEA space-saver, or the retired bridge table, just make the space functional. Arrange your space so that your coffee cup doesn't sit on top of your print-outs, and so that your favorite picture of your pet isn't crumpled behind your reference books. The little things are important for motivation! Maintain a clean and uncluttered writing surface. You'll be switching folders, pulling papers, and taking notes, and you'll want as little confusion as possible.

If you are one of the many who share a home-computer system, establish your workplace around that desirable machine. Talk to family members about moving the computer to the corner of one of the quieter rooms. Perhaps they'd consider putting it in your bedroom. Simply make sure that your workspace is in a place where you can concentrate. Quiet makes a difference; it can double your progress and reduce your stress levels. A good environment is crucial to good work.

Then, gather some tools—pens, red pencils, highlighters, notepads, sticky pads, envelopes, computer paper, and print cartridges. A healthy stash of office supplies is a great motivation trigger. (Buying supplies in office-size packs will keep the cost down.) One of the keys to a successful publication process is having what you need at your fingertips. Prepare for the process; it will go much more smoothly.

A file system is definitely necessary. Invest in a small, roll-away file drawer or a portable file-holder, if you don't have a cabinet available for use. If necessary, you can even use a deep cardboard box or plastic trays. Regardless, buy yourself a big box of manila folders and start stuffing. Use section dividers for advanced organization. For example, devote one section just to your poetry. Then start a new section for research data, notes, submission guidelines, etc. You should arrange your files according to how you feel most comfortable. Here's just a sample of a system: poetry; research information on publications; sample cover letters; submission-package copies; response letters (rejections and acceptances); and materials for packaging, including envelopes, labels, etc.

Also, carve out a space for resource books and magazines, binders of photocopies, a good dictionary, and perhaps your favorite poetry book for inspiration. This small library will be central to your success. Finally, make sure your work area is well-lit. You don't want to encourage headaches and eyestrain that will leave you wanting to throw the towel in early. If you follow these simple but strategic tips, you'll be off to a great start.

REVIEWING YOUR WORK

The final step in preparing for the publication process and achieving your short-term goal is to review your own work again. Carefully select the poems that you feel are at their best; choose the pieces in which you are most confident. Then, subject the poems to heavy critique by yourself and by others. Here are a few ideas on how to conduct these reviews.

Reading Aloud

Read your poetry aloud to yourself. That's right—get up and perform in front of yourself. Does the rhythm flow as well as you thought it would? Did you have to repeat any lines because of awkward phrasing?

Next, have another person read your work to you. Choose someone who enjoys poetry and has some experience reading it. You don't want your brother sighing in the middle of your masterpiece, or your spouse saying, "Wait . . . Honey, what does *that* mean?" If you get a good sport to read the work, hearing the words aloud will help you reconsider the rhythm, the patterns, etc. When you've worked on a piece for so long, you can't sufficiently judge its effectiveness by silently reading it off a page.

Requesting Writing Group Feedback

A writing group is a healthy place to try your poetry out—that is, a constructive and committed writing group. If you do not belong to one, consider the idea. In a writing group, you will find people who are truly interested in literature as art, and

> **Helpful Hint**
>
> Read your poetry aloud. Furthermore, have someone else read your poetry to you. This will help you to identify awkward phrasing, ineffective pauses, breaks in rhythm, etc.

fellow writers who are supportive about the tough road to publication. For helpful advice on writing groups, see page 127.

Attending Open-Mike Poetry Readings

If you don't panic at the thought of performing, take your poems to poetry-reading night at a local café or bookstore. There, many poets gather to expose their work for criticism (hoping that most of it will be positive) and to be inspired by other writers. The audience should be generally supportive. Many people will be in the same boat, and they will figuratively hold your hand and get you through. However, prepare yourself for some honest feedback. If you are looking for constructive criticism, you may find it. And it might not feel "constructive" at the moment. No matter what, it is good to seek reviews from objective listeners. Again, you cannot always be your own best judge.

CONCLUSION

By the time you finish the questions and guidelines suggested in this chapter, you will have cultivated a realistic approach to poetry as a field; you will have better shaped your goals; and you will have organized your time and space so that you will be as productive as possible. Finally, you will have reviewed your work and confirmed that you are ready to market a number of poems. Now it is time to get acquainted with publishing as an industry. Chapter 2 will discuss the various types of publishers that work with poets, as well as the best types of publications to target.

CHAPTER 2

$\mathcal{U}$NDERSTANDING PUBLISHING AND ITS PEOPLE

Publishing, as an industry, can be confusing to the new-comer, and even to those who have already pushed through its doors. There are quite a few terms and titles with which to become familiar. For example, what is the difference between a commercial publishing house and an independent press? Moreover, what is a subsidy press? And there's no doubt that you know what books are, as well as what chapters are, but do you know what a *chapbook* is?

Having a functional knowledge of the publishing industry will allow you to feel in control as you submit your poetry for publication. Even though it might not seem like it, there are a lot of publishers out there. The different types of publishers offer different strategies for getting your work into print. It is important to realize one thing: you *can* get your poetry published, but there are good ways and bad ways to do it. This chapter will spell out the basics—what kind of publishers to stay away from; what type of publications you should initially target; and lots more. If you want to be more savvy than scared, more in tune than intimidated, get to know the following information.

The Three P's: Publishers, Printers, and Presses

The many terms of the publishing industry can set the newcomer into an uncomfortable state of confusion. Don't worry—a couple of general definitions will give you a functional understanding of what you need to know. Let's discuss three words that you are bound to come into contact with over and over again: publisher, printer, and press. You may have already found yourself wondering what the difference is between them, if there is a difference at all.

The term *publisher* generally refers to a business or person whose services provide what is necessary to get a piece of writing into professional print. This means the production of the work in typeset form, the actual printing of the work, the preparation of a cover, and the binding. (Some publishers own their own printing facilities, while smaller publishers simply work closely with one or more printing companies.) The traditional use of the term *publisher* also entails editorial work, as well as marketing, storage, and distribution services.

However, as this chapter explains, many different types of publishers have popped up over the years, and some handle only certain parts of the publishing process. For example, a vanity press may refer to itself as a "publisher" because it produces books. But such a company offers no editorial services, no marketing, no storage, and no distribution. It simply produces the piece of writing in book form for a fee. If you choose to work with such a publisher, you have to rely on your own skills, time, money, and connections to take care of what traditional publishers have considered "the whole package."

Now, what is a *printer?* Yes, the printer is that machine at home—and the one at work—that always breaks when you need it most and always seems thirsty for more ink. But in the larger perspective, a *printer* is a facility that does the actual page production of a work of literature. Many printers are independent companies that do all sorts of projects, from fliers to posters to self-published books. Self-publishers can find good deals by shopping around and comparing costs of various independent printers.

Press is a term that has come to be used interchangeably with publisher. In fact, many publishers (especially small-scale publishers) use it in their titles, such as Copper Canyon Press (a small publisher) and Vantage Press (a subsidy publisher). The original use of the term *press* was a shortened form of "printing press." Now, the term can define any printing or publishing facility. So it can cover both of the terms described above.

After this discussion on these three terms used loosely in the business, you probably realize that the best thing to do is to fully research any outfit before agreeing to work with it. Publishers might call themselves presses; printers might call themselves presses; so presses can be publishers or printers. It's a good thing that writers like to play with words!

TRADITIONAL BOOK PUBLISHERS

Traditional book publishers are also referred to as *royalties publishers*. They are full-service companies, providing the following: editorial work; proofreading; indexing (if necessary); typesetting; printing; binding; marketing; publicity; storage; and distribution. Payment to the author is made in *royalties*—payments predetermined by contract and involving a certain percentage of the profits that the publisher makes on the book. The category of traditional book publishers can be further divided into four subcategories: large book publishers, mid-sized book publishers, small book publishers, and nonprofit book publishers.

The size of publishing companies is defined by sales volumes. A large publishing house has annual sales of $50 million or more. A mid-sized company has annual sales of $10 to $50 million. And a small company has annual sales of $10 million or less.

Large and Mid-Sized Commercial Publishers

You know who they are—the big New York outfits such as Random House, Simon and Schuster, Penguin Putnam, and McGraw-Hill. And many larger publishing companies are currently being bought by even larger conglomerates such as Bertelsmann and Pearson. The industry of publishing has gone merger-crazy, which makes the whole business more challenging and more competitive. Therefore, larger publishers primarily purchase manuscripts by well-established authors and manuscripts that promise to be very lucrative. That rules out the majority of submitted poetry books.

Large and mid-sized publishing houses generally pay the author 5 to 15 percent of the book's selling price as royalties. These larger corporations can also afford to give the writer a sizeable amount of money up front, in the form of a *royalty advance*. For example, the publishing house might give an author $10,000 upon contracting the book, usually contingent upon receiving part or all of the manuscript. This amount will serve in replacement for the first $10,000 the author would have made in royalties, and once profits reach a high enough point, further payments will come in the form of royalty checks.

Royalties can based on *retail price*, which is the price printed on the book; or on *net price*, which is the price that is actually charged by the publisher to the customer, and is often lower than the retail price due to discounts. Royalties based on retail price generally range from 5 to 10 percent. Royalties based on net price generally range from 5 to 15 percent.

Most commercial publishers must accept any product that does not sell in bookstores as "returns." Therefore, they don't gamble on books that won't quickly appeal to a sizeable audience and guarantee worthwhile profits.

Publishing with a larger book publisher offers financial benefits to the author and a good quality product. First, the author is not asked to take part in any monetary investment. She usually does not contribute to costs for production or printing. She does not pay the public relations director or the marketing staff. The financial burden is on the corporation. Second, these publishing houses have enough money to do their job well. Third, larger companies have well-established systems of distribution based on years of experience. In addition, the marketing staffs, publicists, and distributors carry out well-coordinated campaigns. The corporations' well-known logos carry a lot of weight in the industry. Books produced by commercial publishers end up in almost every major bookstore and library. They are more likely to be reviewed by critics at major newspapers, magazines, television shows, and radio programs. All the attention can help to sell books.

Now, here's the downside. First of all, major publishing houses don't publish much poetry. They also do not publish much material that hasn't been either solicited from or sent by an agent that they respect. So, a poet must be well-established, armed with a list of many smaller publication credits and perhaps prior book deals, before even thinking about working with such publishers. Keep in mind that large and mid-sized publishers have to buy back whatever product doesn't sell in the bookstores. So they are not willing to gamble with a questionably marketable book. All of this will also figure into the size of any royalty advance that might be negotiated at the time of contract, so those large advances you might hear about celebrities receiving are not a reality for most writers. You'll find poetry books by Jimmy Carter, Jimmy Stewart, and other renowned people among the works produced by commercial publishers. However, you are not likely to find a poetry book written by a member of your writing group or your PTA on that list. So this area of poetry publication is the very last step in the process, and is rarely ever reached.

Small Commercial and Nonprofit Publishers

Small publishers do not compete with large and mid-sized corporations for the biggest deals. But they may make enough money to employ a small to medium-sized staff, to offer their authors nice royalty packages, and to produce ten to fifty titles per year. These publishing houses are usually privately owned and run. Nonprofit publishers—which include university and foundation presses—can also be included in this category. Nonprofit presses rely on grants and awards from arts organizations, donations, and, often, volunteers or part-time staff members. In his online article, "Independent Presses and the Future of Contemporary American Literature" (www.litline.org/html/harris2.html), Charles B. Harris argues, "Indeed, over the past five years more books of poetry were published by nonprofit literary presses (including University presses) than by all the commercial presses combined." These publishing houses do not choose manuscripts according to pop-culture trends; they are looking for quality niche literature.

Small publishers, nonprofit publishers, and university presses generally have more attainable acceptance processes. Most will give consideration to writers whose names are not familiar to the general public. Furthermore, most of these publishers don't require agents to serve as middlemen. They rely on their own editorial staff to review numerous submissions and choose the ones that fit their style best. In addition, literary editors for some of these types of publishing houses scout for new writers in literary magazines and journals.

But here, too, there is a reality check. These publishing houses can't do the job of publicizing books that the larger houses can, simply because they don't have the money or the connections. So the amount of royalty and royalty advance (if any) that the author receives will not be as high. And poetry collections are not big sellers to begin with. However, if a press is interested in poetry books as part of its literary endeavors, it may be will-

An independent publishing company is usually a privately held commercial company that is owned by one or two individuals who run the company directly. It differs from a publicly held publishing company in that it directly reflects the interests of the owners.

A university press is affiliated with an institution of higher learning. While university presses are nonprofit, many compete with commercial publishing houses.

A foundation press is often an extension of an established foundation, and champions the cause of that foundation. These presses, too, are nonprofit, but few compete with commercial houses.

Helpful Hint

A poet should consider putting efforts toward publishing a book only when she has gained numerous publication credits through literary journals and small magazines.

"Saddle-stitched" or "saddle-stapled" refers to a type of binding. Imagine that you have several sheets of paper. Pile them up and fold the packet in half. Then you have what looks like a book. If you took a stapler and inserted staples at several places along the crease that serves as the soft "spine," the book would be saddle-stitched.

ing to print up to 2,000 copies of a poetry collection. That's a big deal! Yet keep in mind that there is a very limited number of small presses that work within the realm of poetry publishing, compared with the total number of small and independent publishers out there. You need to investigate the individual houses and find out which of these target upcoming poets.

As evident from the information thus far, a poet has a much better shot at publishing with a smaller publishing house than with a larger publishing house. Still, a poet should consider putting efforts toward publishing a book only when she has gained numerous publication credits through literary journals and small magazines. Working with book publishers should not be part of the beginning poet's short-term goals.

Just a few examples of quality small publishers that work with poetry are: Coffee House Press in Minnesota; Copper Canyon Press in Washington; BOA Editions in New York; and Arte Publico Press in Texas. As evident from the locations of these presses, smaller publishers are found all over the country. Small publishing houses differ widely in the selection of material and the quality of product, however, so it is important to conduct thorough research on many different publishers before submitting a manuscript for review. Regardless of their differences, all of these publishers deserve credit for bringing poetry to our culture and our bookshelves.

Some small and nonprofit book publishers do produce a type of publication that is a step down from a full-length book— the *chapbook*. A chapbook is a small volume of poems, usually ranging from ten to fifty pages (depending on the publisher's preferences) but averaging twenty-something pages. Chapbooks are generally saddle-stitched and have card covers. They are not expensive to print, and publishers that offer this option usually allow very small print runs, such as fifty copies.

The quality of chapbooks varies as much as the publishers who produce them. Some are photocopied, while others are professionally printed. Also, some chapbook publishers are willing to include illustrations and/or photographs, while others don't invest in artistic perks. Chapbooks are sold for a couple of dollars—about $3 to $8—not usually in bookstores, but through the mail, after poetry readings, and at literary festivals. They aim to expose lesser-known poets, not to bring in profit. In *Poet's Market*, editor Chantelle Bentley explains, ". . . a chapbook is a safe way for a publisher to take a chance on a lesser-known poet."

There are quite a few small publishers who run chapbook contests. This is a great option for the emerging poet. (For more information on contests, see "Consider Contests" on page 43.) Some poets even self-publish chapbooks, while others unfortunately turn to subsidy and vanity presses. These different types of publishing houses are described in the following sections.

Some chapbook presses publish solicited manuscripts only. However, there are plenty of publishers who accept unsolicited chapbook submissions and/or who run open chapbook contests, as well.

SUBSIDY PUBLISHERS

Subsidy publishers are sometimes referred to as *cooperative publishers* or *joint venture presses*. This type of publishing involves monetary investing on the part of both the author and the press. It is usually agreed that the author's money will contribute to the printing and binding costs. However, subsidy publishers are infamous for overcharging the client. While there are some upright subsidy presses, they are very few and far between.

Because this type of publisher does invest *some* money in the individual projects, many subsidy houses employ editors who read the submitted manuscripts carefully and choose the ones that are most promising. Therefore, acceptance is not a sure bet. After a manuscript is accepted, the publisher usually provides editorial services, warehousing and distribution, and limited publicity efforts. But most often, subsidy presses are not reputable enough to sell their products to bookstores and libraries. In fact, most bookstores and libraries refuse subsidy-press books, as subsidy publishing has a reputation for fraud, dishonesty, and shoddy work.

Also, subsidy publishers tend to be royalties publishers (see

Take Note

Most subsidy presses require unfair amounts of money from the author, turn out low-quality products, and don't keep up their end of the deal. Making back your investment—let alone making a profit—is rare.

Many poets feel they have to resort to subsidy publishing. This is not true. The better bet is to self-publish, thus avoiding ruses and maintaining dignity.

page 27). As a result, if you sign with a subsidy press, that company owns your book. Do not make the mistake of thinking that the copies are yours because you paid printing fees; the publisher warehouses them until they are sold. It is doubtful that most of these publishers even print the number of books that they promise. They will charge for large print-run expenses, but probably will not print many books at all.

In reality, it is very rare that an author makes a profit from a subsidy-published book; often, the author loses money, not to mention time. The deal made between author and publisher involves a shared responsibility to publicize the book. The publicity that a subsidy press conducts is often limited to a couple of ads in writers' magazines and the writing of a press release for the author's book. A press release is simply a summary of the book, with information broken down into clear, appealing sentences. Writing a press release is the easy part. The catch is that the author has to find where to send these press releases, so she must contact media offices at radio and television stations, newspapers, bookstores, etc. Similarly, the subsidy publisher may create postcards with which to announce the book, and promise to cover mailing and postage. But the author has to supply addresses, which means doing the research. In the end, such postcards are rarely effective. It's simply a tactic that the subsidy publisher uses to make the deal seem like a decent package.

Take Note

✖✖   *Stay away from publishers who: require reading fees; make sweeping promises; give extraordinary praise and no criticism; apply heavy pressure on you to use their services; and don't respond to requests for more detailed information on cost, etc. Respectable publishers do not take money for reviewing manuscripts. Furthermore, they do not need to solicit material via mass mailings and magazine ads. More than enough submissions are available from prospective clients, so they don't pressure writers for business. And finally, upright publishers will answer all of your questions quickly and clearly.* ✖✖

Poets who publish via subsidy presses are not respected in serious publishing circles. It is considered unsavvy, for the most part, to pay a lot for the little you get in return. Not only does the author rarely make the money back that she invested, but to make matters worse, the end product is often low in quality and cosmetically unattractive. Many poets feel they have to resort to subsidy publishing. This is not true. The better bet is to self-publish, thus avoiding ruses and maintaining dignity. See the sections on self-publishing (beginning on pages 34 and 138) for more information.

VANITY PUBLISHERS

Avoid working with vanity publishers at all costs. The disadvantages are even more severe than those associated with subsidy publishing. Vanity publishers do not evaluate and choose manuscripts for their potential. Instead they accept submissions on the mere fact that the authors are willing to pay to get into print. Worse yet, some vanity publishers try to hide their true identities by passing themselves off as subsidy publishers. You cannot be too suspicious when it comes to these guys.

Vanity publishers charge the client for printing, binding, and the use of the company name and logo. Unlike subsidy publishing, the author maintains ownership of the material, and, therefore, gets all the profits. But the catch is that there usually aren't profits. You pay a lot of money for very little service—no editing, no marketing, no storage of books, no public relations, no distribution. Often, you are roped into unnecessary package deals. You can get a legitimate independent printing facility to give you a better price, a better product, and no broken promises. Bookstores and libraries almost never carry vanity press books, and critics shun them.

Some anthologies are produced by vanity presses. You'll find quite a few ads in writers' magazines for such anthologies. The publisher will seek submissions to be included in the project, ask

> ### Helpful Hint
>
> It is very important not to be fooled by the sound of a publisher's name. Many vanity presses hide their true identities by using legitimate-sounding names, such as Esteem Press or Solid Ground Publishers.

Take Note

In the publishing industry, vanity publishing is the lowest of the low. Vanity presses often disguise themselves as traditional or subsidy publishers in order to hook your interest. Fully investigate every press that you are considering, ask lots of questions, and demand straightforward answers.

for a fee—a reading fee or the required purchase of a copy of the finished book—and will then use these funds to produce an overcrowded, ill-designed anthology. No critics review such anthologies; no one is discovered from within their pages. The promises about the anthologies being stocked in major stores and libraries are usually lies.

Publishing through a vanity publisher is considered the lowest of the low. As previously mentioned, many vanity publishers try to hide the fact that they are just that. They pretend that accepted work is carefully reviewed, and often send the submitting authors letters that drip with compliments and promises. When a publishing house solicits submissions via mass mailings, sends you profuse compliments on material you've submitted, requires a fee for reviewing your work, and/or resists answering detailed questions on cost, etc., it is most likely a vanity publisher. Furthermore, most vanity publishers, like subsidy publishers, hide fee information until you are roped in. Then they inflate costs, turn out poor-quality products, and often are involved with a number of heists that involve kickbacks among associated businesses. Stay away. You are likely to end up paying many thousands of dollars and making little, if anything, in return.

SELF-PUBLISHERS

This could be you, your neighbor, your teacher, your student, your parent, your child, your electrician, or your physician. You get the idea. You don't have to be a publisher in the traditional sense in order to be a self-publisher. More and more poets are getting frustrated with the publishing world and are deciding to carve their own paths. And this is not a bad idea, if you have the money, time, and skills that it entails. Some writers receive grants from arts foundations, and the money contributes to the production of the self-published books. Most rely on their own savings.

Fortunately, self-publishing is not frowned upon in the professional writing arena. In fact, such well-respected poets as Walt Whitman and Nikki Giovanni started their careers by publishing their own books. Just a few more prominent literary figures who self-published are Gertrude Stein, Edgar Allen Poe, Ben Franklin, and Virginia Wolf.

Self-publishers do all the legwork on their own, usually while maintaining a regular life during normal work hours, as well. The benefit of self-publishing is that the author *can* choose different companies for different services. She can hire her choice of typesetters (if necessary), her choice of graphic artists (if necessary), her choice of a printer and binder. For example, a self-publisher should do lots of research to find out what printer does the best quality of work for the most decent price, taking into consideration, of course, the size of print runs (or number of books produced during the printing). But she is not at the mercy of prepackaged plans set up by vanity or subsidy publishers. In the end, the self-publisher keeps the rights, the profits, and the control.

The author of a self-published book also has to self-manage all marketing plans, warehousing (which is usually storage in the garage or a large closet), distribution, and advertising. If you have a network through which you think you could sell a book—responsive listeners at poetry readings, contacts at local bookstores and schools, etc.—it may be worth looking into becoming a self-publisher sometime down the road. Most bookstores carry some self-published books, and many reviewers are willing to critique them. Yet it is up to the author to get the books into the right hands. This takes considerable aggression and public relations skills.

As advised in the section on traditional publishers, do not jump into the production of a book. Try your hand at the small-magazine market first, and evaluate the responses you receive. If you do decide to go with self-publishing, be sure to fully research the process. This includes figuring out the legal details

Helpful Hint

It is important to not underestimate the amount of time, knowledge, and money necessary for producing a self-published book. You must be an excellent researcher and an aggressive publicist in order to succeed at this type of publishing.

as well, such as the purchasing of an ISBN number (International Standard Book Number) and registering with the Library of Congress. Dave Giorgio of Buy Books on the Web estimates that the average cost spent for self-publishing a print book is $3,000 to $7,000 dollars. Plus, the author is then responsible for shipping copies out to customers. Some self-publishers report that they have spent less, but it takes true know-how. Make sure that whatever money you invest is money that you can do without.

For more issues to consider when self-publishing, see the section in Chapter 6 beginning on page 138. Also note that there are now printing and binding facilities that print only upon request, such as TLC Printing & Copying, Inc. Many of these companies have websites on the Internet. You can electronically store your manuscript with them, and place an order when needed. Such companies do not edit, design, or market books, nor do they obtain ISBN numbers, etc. They simply print the material and deliver it to you. For information on print-on-demand *publishing* companies, see the next section.

PRINT-ON-DEMAND PUBLISHERS

This is one of the newest areas in publishing. It involves electronic storage of a given manuscript. There are several companies on the World Wide Web that provide this service. For example, Buy Books on the Web is considered a print-on-demand publisher.

Buy Books on the Web's Dave Giorgio explained the process that his company follows, which serves as a good example. The author supplies her manuscript in camera-ready form and pays a set-up fee in order to install the manuscript into electronic storage. The fee varies, depending on the length of the manuscript, the number of photographs, illustrations, etc. Giorgio reports that the average fee is $530.00. All forms of literature are welcome for publication, including poetry.

Once the author pays the set-up fee, she has to concentrate on ways to market the work. Meanwhile, the company will assign an ISBN number, which is required of all books. A barcode will also be assigned, and a web page for both the author biography and the book will be designed and placed on the company site. The book is listed with such large online booksellers as Amazon.com, BarnesandNoble.com, and Borders.com. In addition, the book can be ordered via phone, fax, or e-mail. When a book order is received, whether through retail or wholesale, the requested number of books are printed and bound. They are then shipped out within one to two days. A nice perk is that the author doesn't have several hundred copies sitting in her cellar!

However, it is important to realize how much responsibility is left to the author when publishing with a print-on-demand company. The author is often given printed postcards and press releases from the company, but she must develop her own mailing list or audience for the book. This can be time-consuming and difficult. While the book is advertised on the Internet, consider the odds that a random browser would select it. The author needs to convince an audience that her work is different and worth the money, and that's not easy. It is a real challenge for the poet to make back the money that she invests in her book.

Payments from a print-on-demand publisher, as opposed to a print-on-demand printer, are paid in royalties. Some companies promise high royalties figures, such as 20 percent. But be sure that you look into the details of the royalties package. Royalties can be based on either net sales or retail sales. If based on *net sales*, your royalties are calculated from the various prices actually charged for your book. In some cases, the publisher will have charged the retail price—the price on the cover of the book. In other cases, the publisher will have charged wholesale prices—prices reflecting discounts given to major companies or preferred customers. Quite differently, a royalties package based on *retail sales* pays you as though every book is sold at full price.

ISBN stands for International Standard Book Number. Every book is assigned an ISBN. Purchasing such a number is one of the many necessary details involved in self-publishing a book.

But in such a deal, there is often an added condition. For example, if there is a discount of more than 50 percent on a book, your royalties might then be based on net profits, not retail profits.

There are several things to keep in mind when considering print-on-demand publishing. There are lots of shoddy products out there. Scrutinize what the finished product will look like, from paper, to binding, to the cover, before agreeing to publish with a company. In addition, marketing responsibilities fall on the author's shoulders, and it is rare to sell large quantities of work. Be realistic about the profits you anticipate.

There are companies, such as Books-on-Line.com, that offer two types of publishing: print-on-demand and e-publishing. See the following section for more information on the latter. Here, suffice it to say that e-book publishing involves electronically distributing your book for downloading or on software.

E-PUBLISHERS

When referring to e-publishers (electronic publishers), there are two categories to consider: e-books and e-magazines. You should be more concerned with the e-magazines at this point. It is not wise to spend money and time on efforts to publish a book within the early stages of getting into print, even if it is an electronic book. Why? You'll have no audience to buy your book. We'll briefly discuss e-book publishing nonetheless, just so that you are "in the know."

E-Book Publishers

This is the newest type of book publishing and is presently expanding. An e-book publisher makes the author's book available electronically. It can be downloaded onto personal computers or ordered on software, which can then be read on special readers (hardware).

In some ways, e-book publishing is similar to traditional publishing. There should be no fee to publish the book, if it is sent on diskette or submitted over the Internet. The author is generally paid standard royalties (that is, about 10 percent) on profits that are made. The publisher should handle marketing and distribution to companies and individual customers.

While e-books have not become mainstream items yet, big publishing companies and retailers are getting involved. St. Martin's Press, Penguin Putnam, Random House, and Harper-Collins have produced e-books. Their electronic books are purchased from websites and then downloaded. Barnes & Noble also sells NuVoMedia e-book editions and readers; so does Powell's Bookstore—the first independent bookstore to sell electronic books through its website. So this publishing niche is starting to make its mark.

Presently, many of the promising e-book deals are front-list titles, such as Steven King's latest novels and even Monica Lewinsky's self-told story. These books, obviously published by some of the biggest publishing houses, may be simultaneously released in print and "e-produced." There is not much of a market for poetry in e-publishing yet. But you can imagine that the various literary genres will be more involved with this scene in the future. In the meantime, some writers , in the hope of exposure, want to make their work available—even if for free—through smaller, electronic book services.

There are companies that are presently producing software and hardware that allow customers to not only purchase and read electronically produced books, but even to easily produce them! For example, NuVoMedia has produced Rocket eBooks and accompanying digital readers. What's more, RocketWriter software, manufactured by NuVoMedia, gives authors the technology to produce their own Rocket (electronic) books. The system is usable on PCs, employing common computer programs like Microsoft Word. So readers and writers who use Rocket products can download both texts and web pages, or they can

New technologies are quickly arising on the e-publishing front. Consider, for example, InTech Publishing, which produces digital books. Each accepted manuscript becomes a software program in and of itself, which is then made available through downloading and, in some cases, CD-ROM.

"upload" and present their own work. A software package called RocketLibrarian manages all Rocket transactions. Software is free for downloading off NuVoMedia's website (www.rocket-ebook. com), so writers who don't even own a Rocket e-book and reader can "publish" in this medium.

Technology is developing quickly. For example, Everybook, Inc., has already come out with *three* types of e-book readers. Their EBDR is unique: it has two full-color screens that can be used either to read two facing pages, like a traditional book, or set to provide a notepad on one side and a text page on the other. Obviously, this industry is in its infancy, and we will see a lot of advances within a short time. Meanwhile, e-publishing is not immune to scam artists and shady practices. Some electronic publishers will take on the role of subsidy and vanity publishers.

E-Magazine Publishers

Helpful Hint

Consider submitting some of your poetry to webzines. Submission is quick (no postage!), markets are plentiful, and some e-magazine editors guarantee feedback on your work.

Whether you call them webzines, e-zines, or e-magazines, there are quite a few online publications that function just like print magazines. The publishers are simply people who have an interest in something and want to provide an online space to discuss or share it. Some webzines are managed by individuals, while others are run by staffs.

Anybody can start her own e-zine, and many literature lovers have. There are a great number of literary e-zines, and a good percentage of them include poetry. Moreover, many poetry e-zines accept submissions from new poets. Literary e-magazines are the online equivalent to small literary journals and magazines. They receive plenty of submissions and competition is tough. But for poets who want feedback and exposure, submitting to e-zines is a good option. The market is big and easy to use.

Webzines are nonprofit publications, and their publishers don't offer payment to accepted authors. However, some literary e-zines have been awarded for their quality, and it is respectable for an author to report that she has been "e-published" by them. Of course, online publication is not the same as "being in print," but it is an upcoming venue for literature and a good place to start introducing your poetic voice.

Literary webzines vary in their subject matters and the forms and types of poetry requested. Some request rhyming poetry, while others forbid it. Some want horror and sci-fi poetry; others seek religious/spiritual poetry. Some focus on contemporary styles, while others like traditional sounding voices. They also vary in the number of issues published per year, and in other details. So you'll have to investigate the submission guidelines and e-magazine policies at the websites. For a further discussion of this type of publishing, including examples of good e-zines, see "Use the Internet," beginning on page 136.

MAGAZINE PUBLISHERS

Let's get back to the print world, and away from the publishing of books. Magazines continue to be one of the greatest avenues for literature; they never seem to go out of style, especially the ones with the glossy color spreads and the appealing photography. But, for the poet, there are two distinguishable worlds of magazine publishers: popular commercial magazines and small magazines and literary journals.

Commercial Magazine Publishers

Commercial magazines are a big business, both instigating and celebrating the latest trends of pop culture. But not many commercial magazines publish poetry, although a few poems might appear around the holidays, in theme issues, etc. The publishers of these magazines have staff writers and contracted freelancers who supply most of the material. Some accept unsolicited work

Helpful Hint

In the Poetry Society's online article titled "Submitting Your Poems to Magazines; Advice from Peter Forbes, Editor of *Poetry Review*," we learn that well-known literary magazines like *Poetry Review* are sent approximately 30,000 to 50,000 poems a year (which means that approximately 5,000 poets have submitted their work). Forbes reports that *Poetry Review* accepts about 120 of these. On a good note, each one of the submissions is read. However, it is best to begin the publication process with less competitive literary magazines and journals.

and most pay monetary fees for pieces that are printed. The freelance author must sign a contract stating that the work is not being simultaneously published in another magazine.

There are some commercial literary magazines on the market today. More than anything, it's the exposure in a well-respected commercial or large literary magazine that is priceless. That's why countless poets send their work to *The New Yorker* and *Atlantic Monthly*, two of the top intellectual magazines that run poetry, short stories, etc. Competition is fierce, and undeniable preference is given to already-published poets. The commercial magazine publishers are not looking for emerging voices, so it is smart not to rely on them as a viable market.

Small Magazine and Literary Journal Publishers

In *The Writer's Handbook,* editor Sylvia K. Burack writes, "While poetry may be scant in general-interest magazines, it is the backbone of a majority of the college, little, and literary magazines." This is the best market for poets who want to break into print. Small magazines and literary publications are not the products of large-scale corporations. They are produced by small publishers or by university or foundation presses.

These magazines range from photocopied issues edited by one or two people, to high-quality, printed and bound publications that are the products of full staffs. For example, the *Lilliput Review* is a very small (4.5 x 3.6-inch or 3.5 x 4.25-inch), twelve- to sixteen-page magazine that is laser-printed on colored paper and stapled together. Editions are published irregularly and each press run contains 250 copies. The one editor seeks only poems that are ten lines or less. Quite differently, the *G.W. Review* is a perfect-bound, sixty-four-page, biannual publication. It prints about 2,000 copies of each issue, and employs a paid staff. Copies are sold in the George Washington University community and throughout Washington, DC, as well as mailed to subscribers across the country.

Consider Contests

While you are trying to break into print through various publications, don't ignore the hundreds of contests out there. A lot of small and nonprofit publishers run contests that offer monetary awards and guaranteed publication. Also, literary organizations, such as the American Academy of Poetry, hold and advertise competitions. Some contests even award grants and fellowships!

You can find contest information in market resource books, in writers' magazines, online, and in your local bookstores, college English departments, and libraries. It is important, however, to fully research a contest before entering. The majority of contests require reading fees; these fees are usually just a couple of dollars. But be extremely careful; send for detailed information and look for the contest in reliable resource books. Call writers' organizations and inquire whether they have knowledge of the sponsor. If you do enter a contest and get a letter back that makes sweeping promises but states additional fees, you've found a scam. For more information on contests, see Chapter 6.

You can find a small magazine for just about any style, school, form, or subject of poetry. So there's a home for your work out there. Unfortunately, these types of magazines usually can't afford to pay contributing writers in money. So the majority award their authors with copies of the issue in which they appear. More importantly, the exposure is not shabby. Most small literary magazines have a supportive readership, and editors from some of the larger-scale magazines scope out the smaller ones for fresh talent.

In the *Directory of Literary Magazines,* we learn, "Through literary magazines, writers see their art in print and are given a permanent place in our culture. At the same time, readers may discover new voices and talents and experience a wide range of quality literature which is excluded from or underrepresented in the commercial marketplace." Publishers of small and literary magazines provide forums that would otherwise be close to extinction. Keep in mind that most of the publications do not make large profits, if they make any profits at all. The work is done out of love for creative literature. Therefore, it is important for readers and writers to support these publishers.

CONCLUSION

From the information presented in this chapter, you have learned that submitting to the publishers of small and literary magazines is your best plan. Because that area of publishing offers the unpublished poet and the emerging poet the most promise, this book's system is designed around submission to such publications. Leaping to the production of a book is premature at the beginning of your poetry career. When you have gained enough credits to carry weight with small publishers, then attempt a chapbook or a short-run book with a small press. But for now, let's concentrate on getting individual poems into print. Chapter 3 will discuss how to go about finding the particular magazines that are appropriate for your poetry.

$\mathcal{L}$OCATING POTENTIAL PUBLICATIONS

As you learned in Chapter 2, the best way to break into print is to submit your work to small and literary magazines. The term *small* refers to the fact that these publications are produced by small publishers; it does not refer to the physical size of the publications. While you have identified your market space, you have not identified the specific publications to which you will send material. That takes research, and this chapter will get you started by recommending a number of market-information resources. It also discusses the importance of marketing your poetry to a specific audience.

CHOOSING GREAT MARKET RESOURCES

You will be surprised by how many market opportunities surface once you start searching for publications. All of a sudden, you will become highly aware of the new additions on the literary-magazine shelf at the bookstore and in the library's periodical collection. Even free arts publications on the countertops of local stores and coffee shops will catch your attention. It's a great idea to gather as much information as possible, so tap into all of your sources. But also arm yourself with a couple of thorough, reliable market resources that are professionally compiled. These will save you some investigation time and feed you enough market possibilities to keep you going for quite a while. The sources discussed in the following sections were chosen not only for quality, but for the fact that they can be found very easily—in most bookstores; in most libraries; and on the Internet.

Resource Books

When it comes to identifying poetry markets, a valuable resource book offers the following: the names of numerous poetry and literary publications; ways to contact those publications, and perhaps particular editors; a brief description of each publication's focus; and some information on what the editors are looking for. There are books that go even further, listing available submission guidelines, reporting times, circulation and print-run criteria, and even payment information. The books suggested below are not necessarily alike; some are more thorough than others. But each one is easy to use and introduces the poet to a number of promising markets.

Poet's Market

You can find *Poet's Market* in every major bookstore and library. It is one of the most popular and most detailed resources available. In fact, this text is certainly worth purchasing. The very beginning of the book offers a few tips on the publication process, but the bulk of *Poet's Market* (which is approximately six hundred pages in its entirety) consists of entry after entry of individual markets (alphabetically listed) for poetry. Helpful essays are tucked in here and there, and great resources at the back of the book further its value.

Poet's Market uses simple symbols to offer at-a-glance market information for each listing. A key for the symbols is located inside the front cover of the text. Through this system, you can quickly find out: if a market is very open to beginners, partially open to beginners, or open only to experienced poets; which publications are international; which publications are online or electronic; whether a publication has won awards; whether a magazine is specialized; and more. Presses and magazines are listed within the same section, but you can usually tell the difference by the titles.

For a given publication, you will find the following information: address; phone number; website, if available; editor's name; a general description of the publication and the type of poetry it prints, often including information on formatting, number of pages per issue, circulation, and print runs; and submission requirements. Quite a few entries also include direct advice from the editors, elaborating on special points. Some market listings even offer sample segments of poems, to give you a better idea of what the editors are looking for.

Poet's Market also includes an extensive section on legitimate contests and awards, plus contact information for arts councils in the United States and Canada that provide funding for poets through state and provincial grants. A substantial resource section contains summaries of numerous conference and workshop opportunities, as well as helpful organizations. You'll find suggested publications and websites that would be of interest to most poets. Furthermore, there are consolidated lists of publications that accept submissions via e-mail, publishers who print chapbooks, and publishers who print full-length poetry books. Various glossaries and indexes also enhance this resource; the index that lists markets according to the level of writer that they seek, as well as the indexes based on geographical locations and subject areas, deserve special mention. All in all, you can't find a resource book that is better researched than *Poet's Market*.

Poet's Market, published by Writer's Digest, is an invaluable resource text. One of its greatest perks is that each entry is marked with a symbol to designate whether or not that particular publication is open to beginners.

The International Directory of Little Magazines & Small Presses

The International Directory of Little Magazines & Small Presses is considered a top-notch guide when it comes to probing the best markets for poets. This text offers several hundred pages of listings, which are alphabetically arranged, followed by a Regional Index and a Subject Index. A detailed "key" at the very beginning of the book offers guidelines on how to use this resource, instructing readers that magazines are listed in bold upper-case (capital) letters, while book publishers (presses) are listed in bold upper/lower-case letters. This system makes it easy to identify magazine publications right away.

Individual entries appear in paragraph form. The magazine listings include the following information: the name of the publication's press; the name of the editor(s); contact information, including the address, phone number, etc.; the year the publication was founded; a description of the type of writing that is accepted; comments, including the names of recently published authors; circulation information; the number of issues per year; price; average page count; publication size and method of printing; response time; and more. The information offered in small press entries covers average print runs, how many books are published per year, the type of binding and covers used, and other details on book publishing.

There are many international listings, offering market information for such locations as Europe, Canada, Asia, the Caribbean, the West Indies, Mexico, Israel, India, Malawi, and more. And the details on the scope and reach of each publication or press makes this book a valuable research tool. However, be aware that *The International Directory of Little Magazines & Small Presses* does not report on detailed submission guidelines, nor does it reveal upfront whether or not new writers are welcome to submit to a given publication or press. You can, however, use it as a launching pad for further research.

In order to locate the entries that deal with poetry, turn to the Subject Index and look under "Poetry." You will find an extensive list of possibilities. Also, take a look under specific subject areas in the Subject Index; terms are as specialized as "theosophical," "surrealism," and "storytelling," and as general as the names of countries and states.

Directory of Literary Magazines

The *Directory of Literary Magazines* is a helpful guide that deals exclusively with magazine publications. It is compiled by the Council of Literary Magazines and Presses, which is committed to supporting independent publishing throughout the United States. This resource book organizes magazines in alphabetical order according to titles, and provides information in list-like formats.

The entire book fills about three hundred pages. Each magazine listing includes: the editor's name; the publication's address and phone number, plus fax, e-mail, and website information when available; a list of literary genres published in the magazine; a description of the publication; and the subscription price. A nice addition is the mentioning of several recent contributors to each publication. Further information given in each entry involves annual figures on submissions received and accepted, as well as the publication's policy on simultaneous submissions, the reporting time, the first year of publication, and frequency and circulation data. To help you with coding, a key for abbreviations is found at the front of the book.

Unfortunately, it is necessary to page through the text to find the poetry magazines. There is no subject index—only an index that lists magazines according to their geographical locations. Furthermore, no detailed submission guidelines are provided; you will have to contact the individual publications. But you will find foreign-market listings and an easy-on-the-eyes format that is much appreciated.

> ### Helpful Hint
>
> For each publication discussed, the *Directory of Literary Magazines* provides the names of several recent contributors. Take advantage of this helpful feature; read works by the named contributors to find out whether your poetry is reasonably compatible with a particular publication.

The Writer's Handbook

The Writer's Handbook reminds us that few general-interest magazines publish poetry. For acceptance into the ones that do, competition is fierce. It is best to investigate local and regional publications, and of course, college, small, and literary magazines.

The Writer's Handbook has been used as a resource text for over sixty years. The book is geared toward a variety of literary markets, including the poetry market. Before getting to the section on markets, you will find numerous short chapters that cover topics for writers. Just a few examples of the topics discussed are: how to gather ideas for writing; how to handle rejection; the process of rewriting; and development of setting and characters. In addition, there is a section just for poets. It offers eleven short chapters of advice on enhancing your skills and finding your best poetic voice. You can gather helpful advice and encouragement from the first section of the book, even if you find that only a few chapters are applicable to your own writing career.

The second part of *The Writer's Handbook* divides 3,300 markets into forty-five categories. (Please note that only some apply to poets.) The book promises that no vanity or subsidy presses are included in this section, nor magazines that charge fees to review submissions. Whatever submission guidelines are offered come from the editors, publishers, and directors who oversee the selection process. Details such as whether a publication accepts and/or prefers submissions on disk are mentioned when needed. Moreover, there is a specific market section on poetry publications—you do not have to page through countless entries before finding the ones that apply to you.

The editor explains that very few general-interest magazines accept poetry, and for the ones that do, competition is fierce. But the book does list a few general-interest magazine markets, and then instructs the poet to investigate possibilities in local newspapers. Once this information is covered, *The Writer's Handbook* delves into over thirty pages of market information on college, small, and literary magazines. Each publication entry includes the publisher's name and address; the editor's name; and a description of the type of poetry requested, such as ". . . poetry for college-educated, intellectual readers," or "Poetry for children, six to eight years old, on good health. . . ." Information on monetary payment is offered when applicable—that is, for inclusion in the general-interest magazines. Some entries contain additional information, such as the number of poems to submit. But for the most part, the information is just a start. You'll need to contact the individual publications for submission guidelines.

For your further information, *The Writer's Handbook* includes sections on: literary competitions that offer cash and publication awards for unpublished poems; greeting-card markets; writers' colonies; writers' conferences; state arts councils; and writers' organizations. Through this text, you can find literary book publishers that publish poetry. However, poets are encouraged to enter contests that offer publication as a prize, rather than to submit unsolicited poetry volumes of unpublished work for review.

Ulrich's International Periodicals Directory

Ulrich's International Periodicals Directory has been in existence for almost seven decades. It lists international serials, and is a good resource for poets who want to try their hands at lesser-known and foreign poetry markets. The directory includes several volumes. In the "Classified List of Serials" (usually involving the first three or so volumes), look under the subject of "poetry." You will locate a long list of periodicals and can then look them up according to title.

Each entry offers information on the frequency of publication, as well as the publisher's address and country code. Most entries offer telephone, fax, e-mail, and website information. Many entries list the year when the publication was first printed, and also the number of issues that are produced per year. Some listings are for e-magazines. Details such as literary editors' names are not given, but special features—whether the publication accepts illustrations, for instance—are discussed.

Ulrich's International Periodicals Directory can be found in public and university libraries. The multi-volume collection is used primarily for professional publishing and academic research. Therefore, you might locate markets that are not traversed by the general, freelancing public.

Circulation data is provided if the publisher submitted such material. Each listing should contain a general description of the type of poetry that it prints, and publications that are open to new writers often remark on this fact in the "Description" section. A section titled "Document type" will let you know if there is a specialized audience, such as academics. A key to the abbreviations that are used can be found in the "General Abbreviations" list in a later volume.

Few entries offer all of the information mentioned above. Most contain bits and pieces of the whole. Furthermore, no submission guidelines are listed. But this is a good source for publications that aren't listed in mainstream resource books.

Helpful Hint

✖ ✖ *If you find success through publishing individual poems in small magazines, you will eventually consider publishing a chapbook or poetry collection. Many of the resource books discussed in this chapter offer information on small and independent publishers, and, therefore, will be capable of serving you further. But in addition to such books as "Poet's Market" and "The International Directory of Little Magazines & Small Presses," keep in mind the "Literary Market Place: The Directory of the International Book Publishing Industry" (LMP). This resource contains a long list of book publishers under "Poetry" in the subject index. Furthermore, you can turn to a subject such as "Romance" and find presses that are also on the "Poetry" list.*

Each entry in the "LMP" includes lots of contact information—addresses, names, telephone numbers, e-mail accounts, websites, etc.—as well as data on when the press was founded, a description of its work, the number of titles it prints annually, and additional industry information. The "LMP" is an excellent means of finding out about varied-sized presses that publish poetry books. ✖ ✖

Resource Magazines

There are a couple of writers' magazines that are helpful additions to the poet's resource shelf. These publications periodically offer news on new literary publications, and also routinely list small magazines that are actively seeking submissions. It's a good idea to check them out. While you're at it, you are sure to find some interesting articles on how to hone your craft. Before subscribing to any of these publications, check your local library to see if they are available in their periodicals section.

Poets & Writers Magazine

This sophisticated publication is probably the best writers' magazine for poets today. It contains a wealth of helpful information on publishing as an industry and on writing as an art. In every issue, you will find: in-depth feature articles on successful writers and on the craft of writing; regularly published columns; numerous ads for books, educational programs, workshops, literary magazines, contests, publishers, and publishing services; and a resource section, listing available grants and awards, as well as classifieds.

It is within the "classifieds" section that you will find market opportunities for books, chapbooks, anthology entries, and most importantly, magazine submissions. Usually, each listing will contain the full name and address of the publication, the poetry editor's name, the type of submissions that the editor is seeking, and subscription information. Phone numbers and websites are sometimes provided, as well. In addition to viewing the classifieds, be sure to peruse the magazine's many ads and articles. You might come across the name of a poetry publication that you haven't heard of and that you find interesting. And you're likely to learn about several contests that will advance your chances of publication. For subscription information, see page 155 in the Resource Directory.

Writer's Digest

This highly practical magazine calls itself a "guide to getting published." It contains feature articles; regular columns; ads for books and literary magazines, educational programs, workshops, contests, publishers, and publishing services; and classifieds. In addition, *Writer's Digest* has a section called "The Markets," which provides limited listings.

Although the listings in "The Markets" are not always applicable to poets, the cutting-edge information is worth keeping an eye on. Plus, this section offers information on upcoming contests. Finally, as advised under *Poets & Writers Magazine,* look through the various ads and articles for publication names. You are likely to pick up a few market leads just by regularly flipping through *Writer's Digest.*

Other Magazines

There are additional writers' magazines that are not as widely read but that list valuable market clues. *The Writer* is an easy-to-read publication that contains: articles and interviews; ads for guidebooks, contests, books, publishers, and publishing services; and a section titled "Market News," which details a selection of markets that are listed according to their niches or subjects. You may come across the descriptions of several small magazines that seek poetry submissions. The information is current and specific.

Writers' Journal is another resource magazine. It contains regular columns, feature articles, some fiction and poetry, and a "Market Report" that lists opportunities for a specific niche (chosen per issue). If your poetry happens to be compatible with the chosen theme of the "Market Report," you are likely to find some submission opportunities. Also, a limited "Unclassifieds" section sometimes advertises poetry publications that are seeking submissions.

Internet Resources

The Internet is an invaluable tool for poetry market research. There are many websites that offer cutting-edge news on both print and online publications. The sites recommended below offer particularly good information.

Electronic Poetry Center, SUNY Buffalo
http://wings.buffalo.edu/epc/

The State University of New York, Buffalo, provides a wonderful resource site for poets. This website includes long alphabetical lists of both e-zines and print magazines, and allows you to click on the publication name for more information. Some links go right to the publications' home pages, which offer extensive descriptions of the publications and their submission guidelines. Where a home page is not available, as is the case for a number of print magazines, an information page is offered. Some are more in-depth than others, depending on the amount of data that the Electronic Poetry Center was able to accumulate. Through these linked pages, you can collect the following: contact information; data on the frequency of publication and the issue price; comments; and details on the subject and scope of the publication. Some pages also include editors' names, payment policies, and samples of accepted work.

LitLine: A Not-For-Profit Website for the Independent Literary Community
http://www.litline.org/

LitLine's site lists and provides Internet links to hundreds of small presses and print journals. By clicking on a print publication of your choice, you can be connected with that publication's home page. There, submission guidelines and detailed descriptions are found. Through LitLine, you can also link to literary organizations and other helpful sites. Finally, this resource provides news on literary conferences and events. Please note that this site is not exclusively designed around poetry publications.

Poetry Society of America
http://www.poetrysociety.org

The Poetry Society of America's website offers a wealth of information. You will find everything from the organization's membership details to available awards. This website contains descriptions of and links to journals and literary magazines, as well as small presses. In addition, poet colonies, poetry organizations, conferences, festivals, MFA programs, and other helpful Internet sites are discussed. Use this valuable resource to its fullest by investigating the markets it chooses to highlight. Click on the literary publications that interest you in order to obtain more detailed information.

Web Del Sol
http://webdelsol.com

This site is a virtual banquet for the poet and the poetry lover, offering information on specific print magazines and small presses, e-zines, as well as university creative writing programs. Web Del Sol actually hosts twenty magazines, and publishes poetry on the Editor's Picks page. There are online chapbooks to read, fiction and poetry reviews, news, and links to other great sites and online workshops. For example, you can click into "Writer's Block," which is a space for posting your poems and getting feedback from other writers. Web Del Sol also offers chat rooms and a monthly e-mail newsletter, titled *Electronic Literary Arts Newsletter (ELAN)*.

Read through the synopses on small print magazines and

see if your poetry matches well with any of them. Web Del Sol not only provides brief yet valuable descriptions, but also offers many convenient links where you can find more information on particular publications.

FINDING YOUR AUDIENCE

It is important to examine your own poetry and decide for whom it is most appropriate. Then you can better judge what kind of publications to gear yourself towards. In order to do this, ask yourself: For whom did I write this? What kind of an effect do I want to provoke in the reader? What type of readership would find it most appealing?

Think about it. When a company produces a product, a large amount of time and money goes into promoting that product to the specific group of people who are most likely to buy it. For example, let's say that a baby-product company develops a new type of diaper. You will find print ads for this product mostly in women's magazines (or magazines with a majority of women readers), while the television ads will air during time slots that cater mostly to females (during soaps, morning and afternoon talk shows, prime-time family shows). Quite differently, if a company is promoting a hardy new beer, the ads will run in men's interest magazines, entertainment magazines, and during nighttime television and sporting events. The people in charge of marketing these products direct their time, energy, and budget money into a specific audience after carefully studying the television and magazine demographics.

Your poetry is your product. You have conceived it, developed it, completed it, and revised it. You remember the inspiration behind each poem, and you have very specific hopes for what each poem can create in the reader's experience. So you should have no problem deciding on its direction. In fact, you probably have poems that can appeal to a number of markets or audience types. One of the beauties of poetry is that it is

> **Helpful Hint**
>
> Think of your poetry as a product. Find the audience to which it would most appeal, and then spend your time, effort, and money targeting that specific audience.

Literally Speaking

As you begin to work with market resources, you will come across terms and abbreviations that may be unfamiliar. To help you "uncode" the language of publishing, several common industry terms are defined below.

annually—once per year.

b & w—abbreviation for "black and white," usually referring to photographs and illustrations in a publication.

biannually—twice per year; synonymous with *semiannually*.

bimonthly—once every two months (as opposed to twice a month, which is now preferably described as *semimonthly*).

bio—short for "biography"; some magazines ask submitting authors to include a "short bio" in the cover letter, meaning that a brief description of the author's background and present situation is requested.

byline—the line, on a published piece of writing, that gives credit to the author by listing his name.

circulation—refers to the number of copies distributed per issue. In some cases, this term also refers to the geographical extent of the distribution of copies— regional, national, or international circulation.

contributor's copies—the copies of a magazine or book that are given, as a means of payment, to a writer who is published within it.

copy—the text on a manuscript page; the term is used for text that is typed or printed on a page, but not formally typeset.

copyright—the legal right to exclusive control over the publication, production, and sales of a creative work. Copyright offers legal protection from unauthorized copying or use. It is established as soon as the work is fixed on paper or recorded.

entry fee—monetary fee required in order to have the material read and considered during a contest.

first rights—also referred to as *one-time rights* and *first serial rights;* the legal right to the work's first appearance as published material.

hard copy— a print version of a piece of writing; hard copy can also be stored in a computer, or on disk, CD, or tape.

IRC—International Response Card; a prepaid postage receipt that should be included in a submission package being sent to a publication that is published in a foreign country. This receipt shows that you have paid a preset amount of money to cover the postage necessary for the publication's mailed response. The publication staff can redeem this receipt at the local post office.

ms—abbreviation for "manuscript."

multiple submission—also referred to as *simultaneous submission*; the practice of submitting the same piece of writing to different publications at the same time.

one-time rights—see first rights.

perfect-bound—a type of binding, used in the production of a book or publication, in which the groups of pages are fastened to the cover with an adhesive glue, creating a secure spine.

print run—the number of copies printed per issue.

quarterly—four times per year.

query letter—letter of inquiry to find out if an editor would be interested in reviewing a manuscript. A query letter usually contains a description of the work and is often accompanied by a sample section of the work. Such a letter is required when submitting a book to a publisher, but not for individual poem submissions sent to literary magazines.

reporting time—the period of time within which a publication will review and respond to a submission package.

saddle-stitched—also referred to as *saddle-stapled*; a type of binding, used in the production of a book or publication, in which the cover is stapled to the pages within it.

SASE—self-addressed, stamped envelope.

semiannually—twice per year; synonymous with *biannually*.

simultaneous submission—see multiple submission.

multi-dimensional, usually allowing for several different takes on the subject and theme.

Why is it so important to find an audience to target? So you don't waste valuable time, effort, and money sending your poems to editorial staffs who won't even consider them. Countless editors report that the most annoying, and the most common, rejection case is when an author submits poems that are not particularly suitable for the publication's main readership. In such a situation, the editor is not likely to read past the first few lines of the submissions, and certainly can't accept the work for publication.

Keep in mind that there are two things to consider when marketing a poem. The first is subject matter. Specialized magazines require very specific themes, such as spiritual, nature, or women's subjects. Or take, for example, the *Blue Collar Review (Journal of Progressive Working Class Literature),* which prints only poetry that discusses working-class social issues. Other magazines are not as highly specialized, but do have general subject areas. *Dagger of the Mind* is such a publication; it requests science fiction, fantasy, and horror poetry. Of course, plenty of magazines have no specific subject matters, but may have stylistic preferences.

That brings us to another point for consideration: style. Many publications give specific rules on what kind of poetry they accept: rhyming or non-rhyming; traditional or contemporary; free verse or lyrical; metered or unmetered. Often, the submission guidelines specify a line-limit. Sure, you will find plenty of publications that desire all forms of poetry, such as *Blind Man's Rainbow,* which accepts free verse, rhyme, haiku, Beat, and any other type of poetry. But *The Edge City Review* asks for poetry in traditional forms (sonnets, rhyming verse, ballads), narrative poetry, and satire. It does not print free verse or "greeting card verse." So be aware of what forms, formats, and techniques you employ in your poetry, and keep these in mind as you begin to select publications.

You will, no doubt, end up sending submissions to all sorts of magazines. But having a developed sense of your own subjects and styles, and having a mental picture of who would most enjoy your poetry, will help you make better submission choices in the long run. Also, to help you get an increased understanding of audience, read a number of different types of journals and literary magazines. Page through some academic publications concerned with literary traditions and highly stylized details; then thumb through some of the more artistically experimental and "trendy" magazines. Look at a couple of "period" publications (such as contemporary journals, Victorian-theme periodicals, etc.). Explore formal and less formal publications. Afterwards, review your own work and loosely cate-

Helpful Hint

Choose the markets that best match your poetic voice. Do not try to shape your poetry to a trend or a certain publication style. Your heart won't be in it, and therefore your poetry will not be as effective.

✖ ✖ *Don't simply match your poetry to markets that parallel your style and subject matter; match your poetry to markets that parallel your publication credits and your reputation. In his "Writer's Digest" article titled "10 Secrets of Getting Published," author Marshall J. Cook warns beginners not to dismiss the small magazines in favor of larger national and/or commercial publications. He discusses how a good deal of unpublished and newly published writers send their submissions to the big guns, full of hope and anticipation. For the most part, the writers get rejected and are then likely to throw in the towel. Cook's viewpoint is as follows: "This approach makes as much sense as a Little Leaguer trying out for the Yankees or a beginning violin student showing up at Carnegie Hall for an audition."* ✖ ✖

Helpful Hint

gorize your poems. That way, as you begin the submissions process, you will have a pre-set system for deciding which poems should go where. In doing so, you will get your "product" to the most likely buyers and, therefore, will break into print sooner, rather than later.

A LITTLE MORE ADVICE

Although it will be challenging, resist the temptation to abandon careful research in order to jump-start your submission process. Research strategies will be discussed in Chapter 5. Just for starters, here's a little helpful advice to be applied as you begin to locate potential publications.

Take a Look

Whatever you do, avoid judging a publication by its title. Believe it or not, this is a very common error. For example, if a

The content of a publication cannot be predicted by its title. Titles can be very misleading.

poet writes a series of poems that celebrate the wildlife of Africa, he may be tempted to submit them to *Tiger Beat*. However, he'll be wasting his (and the editor's) time. *Tiger Beat* is a pop-culture, teen magazine filled with snapshots of the latest Hollywood heartthrobs. That's a completely different type of wildlife! A poet cannot truly figure out whether his work is appropriate for a publication's audience without taking a look at the type of poetry the editor selects. So whenever possible, page through a few issues of those magazines to which you may be sending submisions.

Get It Right the First Time

Helpful Hint

When using library resource texts, be sure to choose the most recent editions available.

Many of the market resource books discussed earlier in this chapter are revised annually. Be sure to reference the most recent editions. These editions will contain the current contact names, addresses, guidelines, etc.

Also, realize that some publications have several addresses and editors' names listed in their entries. Larger publications may have separate offices for editing, printing, and marketing, for example. And there may be several editors on staff—an editor-in-chief; a poetry editor; a literary editor; an assistant editor. When this occurs, double-check that you have selected the editorial address and the poetry editor's name. Choose the literary editor's name if there is no poetry editor.

CONCLUSION

You don't have to trudge through urban streets looking for clues about poetry publications. Nor do you have to wait for an "insider" to pass along the name of a magazine that is open to unpublished writers. There are a lot of resources that do a good deal of the legwork for you. As you begin to sift through the many publication names and submission requirements, and as you begin to highlight the good opportunities, keep your target audience in mind. Thus, you will choose more appropriate publications and your submission process will be much more successful. And speaking of the submission process, Chapter 4 will teach you how to create a submission package that will be just what the editor ordered.

CHAPTER 4

PREPARING YOUR SUBMISSION PACKAGE

There is no doubt that your most promising market for breaking into print is that of the small and literary magazines. (Of course, contests are also a wonderful opportunity for the unpublished writer, but because of deadline dates and varied submission procedures, they fall outside the Square One System. See Chapter 6 for more detailed advice on contests.) Before launching your poems into the arena, learn how to prepare your material. What can you do to make your packet both professional and interesting? How can you get the editor to open up to your poetry? This chapter tells you exactly how to arrange the most effective submission package.

The majority of publications appreciate the following: a cover letter; three to five original and unpublished poems; and a self-addressed, stamped envelope for the response. It seems basic enough, but there are lots of details to consider.

Please note that you must read and heed all available guidelines before fine-tuning your submission package to a particular editor. Make sure you take the time to research each publication's requests. There are publications that have out-of-the-ordinary submission rules. For example, some do not desire cover letters. Some ask for more poems than the average. If there's anything unusual about what an editor expects, it will be listed in the submission guidelines that the publication prepares.

THE COVER LETTER

The editors of small and literary magazines or journals are usually bombarded with more submissions and responsibilities than they can sanely handle. And many of them do their work for the love of poetry, taking little or no pay. Understand that these are real people, experiencing anxiety, time constraints, and personal preferences. So the best thing you can do is treat them with professional respect and concern. Try to make your cover letter both interesting and direct. Realize that the editor will start observing your writing skills and getting a feel for your voice from the get-go. Most importantly, observe any special requests that have been made in the submission guidelines.

Standard Formatting

When composing a cover letter, the first thing to keep in mind is that the letter should be concise and tailored to the reader's interests. A one-page letter is most preferable. If you gain a lot of publication credits, your letter may eventually spill onto a second page. While this is acceptable, it is not often appreciated. So do make an effort to keep your cover letter down to a page. A wordy, dense letter tends to frustrate the editor, possibly even turning her off from your work.

As mentioned above, keep your individual reader in constant view. You have done your homework and know what the particular publication is like. You have a feel for the target audience. So address the editor's specific needs. Briefly describe your work in a way that shows you share in the style of the publication. Make it known that you are familiar with the publication and are confident that your poetry is appropriate for it.

Type your letter on good-quality white paper. Never print or type on both sides of a sheet of paper. Use a clear, dark, professional-looking font and type-size. Times New Roman font and 12-point type are the most basic choices and widely used in business. Set margins so that they are 1.0 inch on the top and bottom of the page, and 1.0 to 1.25 inches on the left and right. A professional letter should be single-spaced. However, there are places, according to the parts of the letter, where you should skip a line. The standard composition is as follows: the date placed along the left-hand side of the letter, followed by a blank line; the editor's name and title, followed by the publication address, followed by a blank line; the salutation to the editor, followed by a blank line; the four-paragraph body of the letter (as discussed in the following pages) with a blank line between each paragraph, if you choose; the closing and signature, followed by contact information. See the sample cover letters on pages 75 to 85.

Helpful Hint

Today's word-processing programs offer numerous fonts and type sizes so that writers can stylize their documents. But when preparing a submission packet, readability and professionalism should take priority. Times New Roman font and 12-point type are generally accepted as the professional standard.

The Salutation

A polite salutation to the editor will address her by name, if possible. The names of current editors can be found in good market resource books such as *Poet's Market* and *The International Directory of Little Magazines & Small Presses*. If you don't have the name of an editor, you can call the publication office and inquire whether there is a particular person to whom you can address your letter. Sometimes a panel of editors decides on the accepted poems. If this is the case, or if there is no available name, the best salutation is: "Dear Poetry Editor." For a broader spectrum magazine or journal that includes many genres of literature and doesn't list a specific poetry editor, you may want to use the title, Literary Editor.

Poets to Parallel

✖ ✖ *The first paragraph of your cover letter should provide the editor with a broad idea of your poetic voice. One option for making a clear portrayal of that voice is to parallel your work or writing style with that of a well-respected, well-known poet. Of course, you'd want to mention a poet who would suit the publication. In other words, avoid paralleling yourself to an early-American poet if the publication looks for beatnik poetry.*

You will accomplish two things by paralleling your poetry to that of a poet whose work is compatible with the publication. First, you will demonstrate that you are a reader, as well as a writer, of poetry. You are familiar with the field and appreciate other artists' work. Second, you will subtly ask the editor to immediately start anticipating your work. She will be curious about how your techniques match up with, or are influenced by, the writer you have selected to represent you, so to speak. If she likes the poet you are paralleling, you're in luck. She'll be eager to read it. Try to play it safe—if you are very unsure whether or not a particular poet's work would appeal to the publication's audience, don't reference that poet's name. ✖ ✖

Helpful Hint

The Introductory Paragraph

The introductory paragraph should state your request and supply a general description of your poetry, including titles. First, explain that you have enclosed several poems for the editor's consideration. Then name the works, preceding or following the titles with a phrase that captures the strengths of your writing. For example, you might state that your poetry is humorous and accessible. You may want to parallel your poetry to that of a famous poet who has had a major influence on your work or with whom you simply share style—for example, "The influence of Ogden Nash's clever and witty poems is apparent in my writing," or "I write with wit and punch, using a style similar to that of Ogden Nash." Aim for approximately three well-structured sentences. Keep in mind that a paragraph should by no means be comprised of one sentence. And for the sake of space, your introductory paragraph should not exceed four sentences.

Also, avoid sounding arrogant. You walk a thin line by stating, "My work is comparable to that of the great Walt Whitman." Instead, just explain that the influence of Walt Whitman is evident in the poems you are enclosing, or that you write in the aggressive and free-verse style of Walt Whitman. Below are listed several poetry themes and styles, as well as some suggestions of poets who demonstrate them. One may come in handy in your cover letter.

African-American voice:
Maya Angelou; Nikki Giovanni; Melvin Tolson

Allusion (heavy mythical and biblical references):
William Butler Yeats; Samuel Taylor Coleridge

Asian-American voice:
Timothy Liu; Carolyn Lau

Confessional:
Robert Lowell; Theodore Roethke

Contemporary:
Mark Doty; Margaret Atwood

Distinctively American voice:
Walt Whitman; William Carlos Williams

Documentary poetry:
Susan Howe; Ezra Pound

Haiku:
Matsuo Bashō; Yosa Buson

Humorous rhyme:
Ogden Nash

Irish voice:
Seamus Heaney (Irish experience)

Jewish voice:
Yehuda Amichai, Irving Feldman

Latino/Latina voice:
Gary Soto; Alma Villanueva

Love/romance:
John Donne; Elizabeth Barrett Browning; Pablo Neruda

Modern abstract:
John Ashbery; James Schuyler

Musically influenced:
Langston Hughes (jazz/blues rhythms);
Wallace Stevens (lyrical)

Native American voice:
Linda Hogan; N. Scott Momaday

Nature themes:
Ralph Waldo Emerson; Robert Frost

On art and life:
Marianne Moore; Emily Dickinson

Religious/spiritual:
Gerard Manly Hopkins; William Blake; Kahlil Gibran

Social critique/political themes:
Allen Ginsberg; Adrienne Rich

Women's issues (family, sexuality, health):
Anne Sexton; Sylvia Plath

The Second Paragraph

Use the second paragraph to appeal to the editor's interests and ego. She wants to read work that has been carefully selected for that particular publication. For an editor, one of the most annoying situations is spending precious time on an author who submits inappropriate work. Make sure the editor knows that you have done your homework, that you respect her time enough to have included poems that are well within the publication's focus. In three to four sentences, discuss the audience that your poems target, and your understanding that the particular publication's audience is one and the same.

The Third Paragraph

The third paragraph of the letter's body is a place for you to talk smartly about yourself. It's the space to turn yourself into a person in the editor's eyes, not just a couple of sheets of paper. This paragraph is heavily dependent on your particular life—your experience, your education, your profession, etc. If your poetry stems from your experience as a mother, include that you are a mother of four (or whatever the number may be). If you write on the passing of life because you are a physician who has seen life slip away before your eyes, put that in the letter. This is not to suggest that you reveal your family tree and then supply your curriculum vitae. However, do allow the editor to poke through the page and see you. She is human too, and will appreciate forming some kind of mental image of the poet she is about to read.

If you have publication credits—that is, if you previously have been published in magazines, books, newspapers, etc.— name these achievements in the third paragraph, as well. Definitely choose the best of the credits you have. Don't feel that you have to limit these credits to poetry publication. For example, if you have had a short story or a feature article published, go ahead and mention it.

> ## Helpful Hint
>
> Now is a good time to turn on the charm. Show respect and admiration for the editor's work by demonstrating familiarity with her publication.

Of course, stay away from situations in which you paid to be included in an anthology, or stories about how you wrote the sports news for your high school paper. Don't mention any work you've done with vanity presses. Use your professional sense when deciding on what to include. If local newspapers and publications are what you have under your belt at the present time, it's okay to mention them in a sophisticated manner. But literary publications are received much more warmly. Once you start receiving these credits, definitely add them to your third paragraph. One thing you shouldn't worry about is the fact that *The New Yorker* or *Atlantic Monthly* doesn't fall on your list. You have to build your reputation as a poet brick by brick. Editors of small magazines are very aware of how difficult the market is.

You don't have *any* previous publication credits? Don't fret. Many small publications welcome the unpublished writer. Just be sure that you choose such magazines when marketing yourself. And when sending your work to magazines that particularly invite unpublished writers to submit, don't hesitate to mention how much you appreciate their endeavors to expose new poets.

If you have received a higher degree in creative writing, literature, the fine arts, or another applicable field, add that detail to your third paragraph. If you teach poetry and/or writing, that's a good thing to mention. If you have attended well-recognized workshops, have been awarded grants and/or legitimate contest titles, or have studied under a significant poet, include such valuable information. But be careful to avoid putting your resume in this paragraph. Some writers have a tendency to believe more is better. When dealing with submission packets, be brief and to the point.

The Fourth Paragraph

Finally, the fourth paragraph serves as a conclusion. Wrap it up in a polite manner, thanking the editor for her time and valuable

Helpful Hint

When submitting to a publication that is particularly open to unpublished poets, it is a nice touch to mention your appreciation of this fact in your cover letter. Thank the editor for her help in providing opportunities for new voices.

review. Mention that you have included a self-addressed, stamped envelope and that you look forward to receiving the editor's response. You may even offer to send additional work upon request. Keep this paragraph short and sweet.

The Closing and Contact Information

Your closing should maintain the respectful and professional tone of the letter. A simple, "Thank you" or "Thankfully" is just fine. The following closings are also appropriate: "Sincerely," "Many thanks," and "Respectfully." The line below should contain your signature, which should lie immediately above your typed-out name. You can provide your contact information below your signature. This includes your mailing address, phone number(s), and e-mail address. Traditionally, this information can be listed at the top of your letter instead, in the upper right corner. However, most of us have multiple phone numbers and addresses to list these days. Aesthetically, it is more pleasing to provide the details at the bottom of the letter. It simply will look awkward if you have eight lines worth of contact information at the top of your very important letter.

The little details count. An editor can make a judgement on your professionalism simply by the way you physically format your letter. And she wouldn't be so wrong in doing so. After all, a good poet has a strong sense of what is visually pleasing and effective. A large part of a poem's power is derived from the way text is laid on the page. Your cover letter should be viewed almost as a poem unto itself!

After you have finished writing the letter, proofread it. The importance of proofreading cannot be overstated. Computerized spelling and grammar checks are not infallible. Then, set your page up so that the letter falls nicely within the space of the paper. If your letter appears a little short for the page, you may want to slightly adjust your margins.

> **Helpful Hint**
>
> Most editors opt to respond to submissions via mail. However, it is polite to offer the additional contact options. Therefore, consider providing your phone and fax number(s) and e-mail address, as well.

Sample Cover Letters

Below are several sample letters for you to peruse. They are each unique in their particular situation. All the names, addresses, even publications and poem titles are fictional. Please do not rely on them as market tips. Also, please realize that these letters are samples to provide you with guidance. Surely, as a poet, you are most capable of composing your own unique and appropriate cover letters. Personalize your letters; make them exclusive to you and your poetry.

For the Unpublished Poet
Sample Letter #1

In the following letter on page 75, the writer briefly discusses her own culture and heritage to catch the editor's interest. She does not have publication credits, but the writer gives depth to her position as a poet by explaining that her work is born from authentic experience. She allows herself to get personal, while maintaining an intelligent posture. Also, the writer makes it very clear that she is a reader of the publication—something that editors truly appreciate.

Helpful Hint

✖ ✖ *Be sure to be professional when writing a salutation to a female editor; do not guess at the editor's marital status by choosing either Miss or Mrs., and then hope to be correct. Simply write, "Ms. _____." This is the most politically correct and least offensive salutation. You will start off on a bad foot if you address the editor incorrectly.* ✖ ✖

(Current Date)

Peter Marco, Poetry Editor
American Rhythms
1881 Lucia Street
New York, NY 12345

Dear Mr. Marco,

Please consider the enclosed poems for publication in *American Rhythms*. You will find three original works that conform to your magazine's style and to your submission guidelines: "Bass in the Basement"; "She Sang to Me"; and "New Waltz." My poetry is written in jazz/blues rhythms and encourages rich visual imagery. I have been influenced by the work of Langston Hughes, and trust that you will recognize his contribution in my poetry.

My work appeals to readers who have experienced Black American culture, and to those who appreciate and desire to learn more about it. Each poem explores sounds and sights, old heritage and new visions. I am fully aware that *American Rhythms* studies how, in poetry, musical rhythms and words work together to move the reader. I am confident that you will find that my work falls within *American Rhythms* interests and scope.

My personal background will give you a better idea of my perspective and desires. I come from an ethnically and racially diverse family. I have always been fascinated with learning how the varied languages and music of my ancestors have made me who I am today. Literature has been a wonderful guide and companion during that exploration. The fact that I would go on to become an English teacher in the secondary school system is, therefore, a logical one. I spend a great deal of time reading and discussing literature, helping young adults to find something of themselves in the works of our great American authors. In the meantime, I, too, have found my voice through poetry. Now, I desire to share it with others.

I sincerely thank you for taking the time to consider my submissions. I have enclosed a self-addressed, stamped envelope, so that you can conveniently inform me of your decision. However, you will also find an e-mail address and phone number below, in case you prefer to contact me using those methods. If I can answer any questions or if you would be interested in reading additional work, please let me know.

Many thanks,

Nicole Freeman
1994 Janice Drive
Laurel, NY 12345
Phone: (W) 123-456-7890; (H) 123-654-0987
E-mail: nifree@guide.com

For the Unpublished Poet
Sample Letter #2

The next letter is a good guide for the poet who knows she is marketable within a very specific niche. Here, the writer has found a publication that would appreciate her particular real-life experience. The poet does not have applicable educational background, nor previous publication achievements. However, she has familiarized herself well with the publication to which she is submitting. She found that it prefers chatty, light-hearted poetry that makes the reader chuckle with a sense of shared experience. The poet's gentle but frank style comes through in the letter, allowing the editor to anticipate such talent in the poetry that would follow.

Motherhood and More

The sample letter on page 77 addresses the timeliness of women's issues in poetry—how writings on such issues as sisterhood and motherhood provide an important support structure for women today. Interestingly, in *Mother Songs: Poems For, By, and About Mothers*, edited by Sandra M. Gilbert, Susan Gubar, and Diana O'Hehir, we learn that motherhood became a popular subject in literature—as far as women writers are concerned—only as recently as the nineteenth century. Gilbert, Gubar, and O'Hehir theorize on why this might be true: "Perhaps . . . because the subject was so often sentimentalized, serious writers rarely turned to it . . . ." Mothers, according to Victorian stereotypes, were supposed to be selfless; apparently, it would be frowned upon if a mother exhibited the "masculine" qualities of "authority and assertiveness" that were thought necessary in order to be an effective poet.

Luckily, by the late 1800s, and throughout the 1900s, women gained greater rights and status, from legal standing, to political and social standing, to education, and so on. Today, women writers celebrate motherhood openly, as well as discuss its challenges and difficulties. In *Mother Songs*, the editors write, ". . . women poets have combined literary creativity with biological procreativity," and American literature is all the better for it. So, if you're a mom, please don't feel that the subject is too sentimental, or too personal; share your experiences and create a niche.

(Current Date)

Marguerite Linyon, Literary Editor
Tea Leaves
17 Executive Boulevard
Bloomton, TX 12345

Dear Ms. Linyon,

Please review the two poems included in this submission package: "Canterbury Kitchen" and "Flowers to Drink." You will find that they are written in conversational style, highlighting the delights and demands of family life. I strive to blend light humor with sensitive concern, resulting in a voice that falls somewhere between Erma Bombeck and Dorothy Parker.

Tea Leaves offers women special support, gentle guidance, and celebratory belief in themselves. Your magazine is well matched to the goals that I set in writing women's poetry. My poetry is for the woman who wants to relax with a cup of tea and some familiar sentiments at bedtime. It is for the woman who wants to catch a few smiles of sisterhood during the commute to work. It is for the young student who wants to probe the rites of passage that women in our society often silently endure.

My sense of womanhood has been influenced by a long history of Southern femininity, and I have had to modernize and remold values and beliefs over time. Furthermore, I am a mother of four and am now entering into the grandparent stage of life. Throughout my experiences, I have found expression and release in writing. In my poetry, I carefully discuss such significant life stages as marriage, motherhood, and aging. Now, I ask you to give me the opportunity to share my work with others. I have been inspired by many female poets throughout my life, from Elizabeth Barrett Browning to Anne Sexton, and quite simply, I'd like to return the favor.

Thank you for taking the time to review my work. I have included a self-addressed, stamped envelope for your use in responding to my submissions. Please contact me if you need any more information or desire additional work. My contact information is listed below.

Sincerely,

Jodie Winterberry
49 Birch Lane Drive
Cantor, VA 54321
Home Phone: 456-123-7890
Work Phone: 456-012-3456
E-mail: jowry@square.one

For the Unpublished Poet
Sample Letter #3

The final sample letter for unpublished poets is particularly helpful for writers who have advanced degrees in applicable fields—for example, creative writing, literature, and the fine arts. Editors respect a writer who is serious about literary endeavors, and participation in a pertinent academic program certainly shows commitment. Similarly, poets who have been enrolled in well-respected workshops and/or conferences should include that information in their cover letters. Observe how a young man, just out of graduate school, can use his recent studies to enhance his status as a writer.

Smart, But Scared

It's no fun to be a new college graduate. Suddenly, you are staring the world in the face, with barely anything in your pockets and only a transcript in your hands. Many new graduates feel shaky and lack confidence, because they feel like newborns in an adult world. It's no different for many poets coming out of advanced creative writing degrees, workshops, conferences, and seminars. They feel, perhaps, academically prepared, but what of the *actual plunge* into the role of poet?

Well, if you find yourself stuck in the mire of self-doubt, remember this: if you have invested your self, your time, and your money in a program that has specifically developed your poetry-writing skills, you'll look pretty good to an editor! Editors of poetry magazines truly appreciate the poet who takes the craft seriously. So you are not starting with nothing. And you are especially well-positioned if you have studied under a successful poet. That's something you can brag about in your cover letter—but don't make it sound like bragging. For example, you could write "I am especially thankful to my mentor and teacher, _____, under whom I studied at the aforementioned conference. My skills have been greatly enhanced by her advice on effective line breaks and creative rhythms. The influence of her successful collections is evident in my submissions." Such an acknowledgement shows your general appreciation of others within the poetry community, as well as your willingness to develop and enhance your craft.

(Current Date)

Jude Kastinski, Poetry Editor
Poet's Pride
30 Steepleton Street
Brickstone, ME 54321

Dear Mr. Kastinski,

Enclosed are four works of poetry for your consideration: "My Own Eyes"; "A Branded Brotherhood"; "Down the Front Steps"; and "Far From Laurel." You will immediately observe my aggressive and free style, heavily influenced by the works of Walt Whitman and William Carlos Williams. I strive to provoke an exploration of the self through everyday, but nonetheless powerful language.

Familiarity with *Poet's Pride* makes me confident that you will find my work appropriate. I find my poems especially compatible with several of the new poets you have published within the past year: James Rhone; Gretchen Neutchen; and Harry Kington. My poetry appeals to those who enjoy vibrant, philosophical writing made comfortable through the use of American vernacular.

Emerson's call for an "American bard" has already been answered by some very powerful voices throughout the past century. As America continues to develop, however, new voices from each generation must step into that role. I greatly appreciate the fact that *Poet's Pride* seeks to introduce new writers to the poetry forum. I recently completed a Master of Arts in Creative Writing at the University of Colorado, and have attended numerous poetry workshops over the past couple of years, including a Key West Writers' Workshop. I have worked diligently on my craft and am now looking forward to the next stage in my writing career.

Thank you for taking the time to review my work. I value your opinion and look forward to receiving your response. Enclosed you will find a self-addressed, stamped envelope for your use. I also list several other methods of contact below, in case you find them more suitable. Please let me know if you would like to see additional work.

Thank you,

Carl Waters
76 Alabaster Place
Philadelphia, PA 45678
Phone: 765-432-1098
E-mail: carwat@signif.com

For the Previously Published Poet
Sample Letter #4

Publication credits always strengthen an editor's impression of a poet—unless the credits are for vanity press books and neighborhood-block newsletters. The following letter skillfully works two respectable publication credits into the third paragraph. Furthermore, the poet expresses a long-term personal interest in the region toward which the publication is geared. Since the writer is familiar with the niche culture and imagery, the editor is likely to gain confidence in the appropriateness of the poems.

On Being A Down-Home Poet

The sample letter on page 81 raises the issue of establishing yourself as a local poet. While it is tempting to target the magazines that circulate on a national level, there is great exposure and satisfaction to be found in writing for and about your old stomping grounds. Chapter 1 addressed how difficult it is for a poet to push her way into the top anthologies and publishing houses. Most of us have to settle for small-scale success, and taking advantage of your local knowledge is a good way to gain it. You already have 101 passions (both good and bad) about your home area. Why not write about them?

Let's look at a poet who never hobnobbed with Robert Frost or Allen Ginsberg, but who made a significant difference to those around him on Long Island. According to *Sounds and Sweet Airs: The Poetry of Long Island*, edited by Joan D. Berbich, twentieth-century poet Simon Sigmund Tanhauser was referred to as the "poet laureate of Long Island." Better known as S.S. Tanhauser, he published from his local area, about his local area. Tanhauser's work appeared in such publications as *The Long Island Forum,* The Long Island Railroad's 1923 commemorative booklet, and in published collections including *Rhymes of the Sunrise Trail* and *Songs of Horticulture*. In his poetry, Tanhauser discusses everything from history, to familiar town names, to the local wildlife. His words are beautiful to hear for any reader, and especially precious to those who inhabit and love Long Island. He serves as a great example of a poet who attained regional success by writing on a subject about which he had a personal passion. So remember, if you keep your local options open, it could open up a much larger world for you.

(Current Date)

Lorraine Essexton, Literary Editor
Rock & Water Journal
Gransburg, RI 98765

Dear Ms. Essexton,

As per the requests in your submission guidelines, I am enclosing five poems for consideration in *Rock & Water Journal:* "The Cape Laughs"; "Round Rocks of Autumn"; "Shore So Shallow"; "My Only Home"; and "Steady Hands on the Waves." The poems are constructed around my personal experience of life in New England and the true American Spirit that resides there. I write in descriptive, non-rhyming verse inspired heavily by the Transcendentalist writers.

Rock & Water Journal is respected for its distinguished editorial eye. Personally, I am pleased to reveal that two of your recently published poets are among my favorite emerging writers: Anne Savior and Ted Tomay. I find kinship with these poets, as we share similar style and subject matter. I, too, wish to celebrate the way that New England—one of the oldest, most traditional, and most beautiful areas of our country—moves the spirit and influences the body.

I started writing regional poetry over fifteen years ago, when I left my childhood home in Concord, New Hampshire, to accept a corporate banking position in the Midwest. Missing the sights and sounds of my first home, I wrote poetry to bring me back. Eight years later, when I returned to the region of my birth and young adulthood, I distributed some of my poetry as gifts. The warm response caused me to continue writing, as well as to seek publication. My work has been printed in two well-respected regional magazines: *Northeast Notes* (April 1999) and *Sand Pipers* (May 2000). I look forward to continuing to work within this niche, and publication in your highly regarded journal would be a wonderful leap in my career endeavors.

I sincerely thank you for taking the time to review my work. Please find a self-addressed, stamped envelope enclosed for your response. I also provide further contact information below. I look forward to hearing from you.

Respectfully,

Michael Oarsman
45 Stonebridge Court
Thatcher, NH 88745
Phone (H): 654-321-0987; (W): 654-321-7890
E-mail: moars@guide.pub

*For the Poet Unpublished in Print,
but Published Online*
Sample Letter #5

Have you, like many other poets, tried your hand at a few web-zines? If so, were you published online? While a lot of e-zines are obscure, homegrown niche magazines, there are also a number of them that have received awards for their editorial choices. If you have had a poem published online by a webzine that is significant in its genre, include that in your cover letter as a publication credit. Granted, online publication is not the same as print publication, but it has already become accepted as a viable way to showcase good writing. Take a look at the following sample letter, which includes information on webzine publication.

Getting Online

For many writers, poetry is something wonderful that exists outside of the harsh world of finance, corporate obsession, trendy electronics, and flashy media. In fact, it's easy to place poetry as the profound "other." In *Can Poetry Matter?: Essays on Poetry and American Culture*, author Dana Gioia writes, "American poetry has defined business mainly by excluding it. Business does not exist in the world of poety. . . . It is the universe from which poetry is trying to escape." We want to keep poetry in its pretty box, but we also have to face the fact that poetry must change with the times. That's why so many poets are now turning to the world of the Internet.

At first thought, it might feel almost sacrilegious to put your poetry online, over an electronic medium that is—yes—flashy, trendy, and out-of-control. But the truth is that many poets have gained great exposure and helpful feedback from webzine sites. It costs nothing to visit, and nothing to submit. And if you get chosen for publication at a well-respected poetry e-magazine, there's no reason not to mention that in your cover letters. The Internet is becoming a significant space for poets, so you might as well jump in. It might take some practice to change traditional notions of how poetry should be presented, but as the old saying goes, "Use what you got!"

(Current Date)

Thomas Campton, Poetry Editor
Creature Calls
56 Red Clay Circle, Suite B
Summit, NM 67890

Dear Mr. Campton,

I am submitting three poems to be considered for publication in *Creature Calls:* "Snakes and Secrets";
"In a Coyote's Ear"; and "Fast the Feet." These nature-oriented works discuss the mysteries and lessons
that the desert lands offer. My poems take the reader on a tour of the North American southwest,
stimulating the imagination through rich descriptions of scents, sounds, sights, and textures.

As part of the readership of *Creature Calls,* I know that your publication focuses on the varied physical
beauties of the southwest. But even more than that, the poetry printed in *Creature Calls* reveals the
spiritual and cultural inspirations triggered within this region. My poems are consistent with your
publication's scope. They explore the paradox of the desert experience—how it forms the individual
by allowing him to become one with the landscape and its life.

I first decided to explore the North American southwest during a brief vacation from the urban craze
surrounding my Miami retail store. To my surprise, I found not only rest, but energy and vision. I have
returned again and again since then, adding continually to a large collection of poetry written specifically
about these journeys. Seeking to share some of these works with others, I pursued online publication in
several appropriate webzines. Among my acceptances, I have had the privilege to publish two poems with
Drops of Desert, which is recognized as one of the most sophisticated and educational online magazines.

Thank you for taking the time to consider my submissions. Your response will be greatly valued. I have
included a self-addressed, stamped envelope for your reply. Please contact me if you would like additional
poems or information.

Thankfully,

George Chiesa
342 Francine Drive
Thornton, FL 87654
Phone: 432-109-8765
E-mail: gjrc342@knowhow.now

For the Previously Published Poet
Seeking Chapbook Publication
Sample Letter #6

Clearly, this book focuses on submitting individual poems to magazines and literary journals. It is geared toward the poet at the start of her poetry career. However, as you follow the Square One System and accumulate publication credits, you are likely to become interested in publishing a chapbook. A chapbook, as discussed in Chapter 2, is a good way for a publisher to assess response to a poet's work without incurring much cost. It is also a good way for a poet to move into the next stage of her poetry endeavors. To get you started on the right foot if you decide to go this route, here is some advice.

Locate publishers who specifically seek chapbooks. *Poet's Market* is very helpful in listing such presses. There are many publishers who regularly publish poetry books, but never do chapbooks. Next, be sure to obtain all possible submission guidelines, including how much sample work should be sent. Some chapbook publishers request only a few poems, while others ask for at least half of the collection. Some like to see that a number of the poems have previously been published, while others like the bulk of the collection to be new work. Finally, read the following sample letter written for chapbook submission. Note that the writer lists the poems that have already been in print, and also tells where they have appeared.

The sample cover letters demonstrate different ways that you can introduce your work to an editor. While some editors choose to read the poetry first, most rely on the cover letter as an introduction to the work. And first impressions are vital. So always write respectfully to the editor, acknowledging your appreciation of her time. Avoid bragging; it is best to sound secure, but not arrogant. Be sure to maintain a professional but friendly tone. Finally, tailor your letter to each specific publication.

(Current Date)

Shannon Albon
Two Window Press
6549 Sandalwood Drive
Smithtale, MN 65432

Dear Ms. Albon,

Thank you, in advance, for considering the enclosed segment of my chapbook manuscript for publication. *Air to Drink* is a sixty-page chapbook telling of a woman's excursions through the streets of various urban centers. In accordance with your submission guidelines, I have included a sample of five poems: "London Toast"; "Canticle of Cement"; "The Children at Lunch"; "The Streetlamps Cried Gold"; and "One Martini." My work contains strong visual imagery embedded in free verse.

I greatly respect the chapbooks published by Two Windows Press. In fact, I decided to submit my chapbook to you after reading Kyle Tanin's *Expression Express* (1998). My collection is comparable to Tanin's work in style and motif. Both discuss the fascinations and the horrors triggered by large-city life, its existential and cultural roller coaster.

I was raised and educated in New York City, where I studied literature as an undergraduate and business at the graduate level. I presently run my own art and book shop there. My business requires that I travel extensively, both inside and outside the United States. *Air to Drink* is borne from magical everyday experiences that I have chronicled in varied locations around the world, including home. I began publishing individual poems from *Air to Drink* several years ago. "Canticle of Cement" appeared in *Northeast Notes* (1999); "The Streetlamps Cried Gold" was published in *Ruins and Resurrections* (1998); "London Toast" was printed in the University of Gates' *Story Words* (1998); and "West Coast Winter" (not presently included) was published in *Time to Place* (1998).

Again, thank you for taking the time to consider my work. I look forward to your response, and will gladly send the entire chapbook manuscript promptly upon request. My self-addressed, stamped envelope is suitable for the return of the enclosed material and your decision, but please feel free to contact me in whatever way you find most convenient.

Respectfully,

Gemma Karolis
4804 E 72 St, Apt BB
New York, NY 01234
Phone: 210-987-6543

SELECTED POEMS

If there is anything exceptional about the layout of your poems—for example, intentional blocks of empty white space; a shape formation with words—alert the editor to this situation in your cover letter.

Now it's time for the fun part, right? I'm sure you are anxious to display your work. When sending poetry out, there is a temptation to go "artsy" and force that editor to see that *you* are different. But the best thing you can do is to follow a few general guidelines and to remain professional. Trying too hard is simply too much.

First, let's take care of the basics. Print or type your poetry on good quality, 8.5 x 11-inch bond paper. The quality of paper is judged by weight (evident through the thickness). Paper that weighs anywhere from 16 to 24 pounds is acceptable, but lean toward the heavier weights. Such paper is thick and sturdy enough to survive contact with numerous hands. It will be professional in appearance and to the touch.

Give every poem its own page, and type or print only on one side. Each poem will be reviewed as a complete work unto itself. When setting the page, establish the format so that you have at least a 1-inch margin all the way around. Setting the left and right margins to 1.25 or 1.5 inches is just as acceptable. Adjust the margins to how your eye best likes the poem. Generally, 12-point type is best to use; it is easy to read and unobtrusive.

If your poem is arranged in a standard fashion—that is, traditional stanzas—single space the lines and leave a double space between stanzas. There are forms of poetry that exist outside this set-up, such as sonnets and haiku. Of course, the poem should be set on the page as you would like to see it printed. Part of the art of poetry is the physical layout. For example, some poets compose shapes into their poems. Some like to communicate a barren feeling by using a lot of empty white space. You don't have to manipulate your art for easy editorial reading. However, if your construction of a poem is somewhat bizarre, such as some of the later works in Susan Howe's *Singularities* collection, mention that in your cover letter. Ask the editor to appreciate the visual meaning, as well as the textual meaning, of your work. Then she won't have to wonder whether your printer went haywire and you didn't have time to proofread.

Be sure to observe the rules laid out in the submission guidelines for each publication. The requested number of poems for review varies from publication to publication. Some ask for up to ten, while others request only two or three. The majority of requests fall between three and seven, but it's not wise to make assumptions. If you don't find a specific number in any of the literature, call or e-mail the editor. By no means send a collection to a magazine that requests individual poetry submissions. Only send a complete manuscript if you are submitting either a book to a book publisher or a chapbook to a press. And even then, some editors prefer just to see a few sample poems. So please do your homework before putting that painstaking package in the mail.

Choose your submissions most carefully, always with the specific publication's audience in mind. Also, keep in mind that most editors despise lengthy, densely arranged poems. Remember that the majority of literary editors are inundated with submissions. It will be an automatic death-sentence for your work if you send a book-length poem to a small magazine or literary journal.

The first (and often only) page of each poem should contain some vital identification information in the upper right corner. You should include, on separate lines, your name and two to three methods of contact, such as your phone number, address, and e-mail address. Then, after skipping down a few lines, provide a title for the poem. Even if you don't normally title your work, you should assign a name to each poem for the editor's convenience in referencing the piece. Also, should the piece be selected for acceptance, you can avoid confusion caused by the lack of a title. Use your own stylistic preferences when deciding whether to center the title of the poem or to run it along the left margin.

Your poem should immediately follow. Unless it will ruin an intentional shape, set the lines along the left-hand margin.

Helpful Hint

Most often, exceptionally long and tightly packed poems are not appealing to editors. They must select poems that fit nicely into limited space, not to mention the fact that it is intimidating and time consuming to read lengthy works.

Allowing poems to float in the middle of the page, with every line centered, is not preferable.

Poet's Market, discussed in Chapter 3, offers some great advice for situations in which additional pages are required for the completion of the poem. Put your name in the top left margin of every additional sheet. (The top margin is referred to as the *header* in most computer programs.) On a separate line, immediately after your name, insert a significant word from the poem's title, as well as a page number, and a notation concerning whether the page introduces a new stanza or is a continuation of the previous one. A simple phrase such as "continue stanza" or "new stanza" is sufficient. There is no need to provide your contact information on continuation pages.

It is a good idea to put a little note on the bottom of the first page of a continuing poem, as well. Utilize the footer (bottom margin) space if you are using a word-processing program. At the right corner of the footer, type in a short phrase like "stanza continued on page 2" or "continued on page 2."

Editors do not like the use of paper clips, rubber bands, or fancy clamps to hold pages together. By providing page numbers on any continuation pages, you should feel confident that your poems will remain intact. Even the use of staples is a turn-off for some editors, although staples are the least offensive of the clip apparatuses. So your safest move is to trust that, with proper labellings, the editor and other staff members will keep your poetry together and in proper order. For a further discussion of do's and don'ts for poetry pages, see the inset titled, "When Trying to Catch the Editor's Eye . . ." on page 89.

OTHER IMPORTANT DETAILS

The following details are a few more examples of how the little things matter in preparing a submission package. If you take the advice seriously, your packet will be in great shape for the editor's review.

When Trying to Catch the Editor's Eye...

In the quest to make your submission package different from the hundreds of others, you might decide to add a creative touch. Most editors don't mind *conservative* creativity. For example, sophisticated textured paper and slightly tinted paper are acceptable. (Avoid obnoxious colors like hot pink and electric blue.) Or, if a poem is about a specific location, you might want to include a high-quality photo of the area under discussion. This is especially appropriate if the publication likes to include photos or illustrations with literary work. Also, you have the option of selecting a font that is slightly different from Times New Roman.

However, don't stray too far from the beaten path and, above all, make sure the material is easy to read. Once you get into stylized font, for instance, you run the risk of distracting the reader from the text. The editor might not share your tastes of what is attractive for print, and you risk using a font that is difficult for some people to read. There's a great danger of doing more harm than good.

Creative is nice; bizarre is dangerous. Realize that trying to be different can get out of hand. Playful eye-catching tactics can easily scare the editor off, or simply repulse her. For example, here's two true and frightening stories. One publisher described a hand-written submission, scrawled out in crayon on pieces of butcher-block paper that had been pasted together. His immediate thoughts were: "This guy could be a criminal." And a book editor complained that she received a submission with magazine cut-outs decorating the pages, not to mention strings of rubber cement from the bad glue job. She rushed through the read just so she could wash her hands! So when in doubt, stick to your basics.

Include a SASE

It is very important that you include a self-addressed, stamped envelope (SASE) for return of your material and the editor's response. All publications ask this of submitting writers. If you don't want the hard copies of your work returned—if you simply want the editor's response card or note—specify to the editor that the documents are disposable. Nonetheless, include a SASE because many editors communicate their responses by mail. Also consider the option of printing up response post-

"X" Marks the Spot

With today's personal computers, it is very easy to make countless copies of our work. Therefore, not many poets desire to have their poem print-outs returned in the mail; a simple "yes" or "no" will do. If you are not anxious to have the print-outs mailed back to you, and if you want to be a little creative, consider the option of having response postcards printed up. (Don't forget to cover the postage!)

First, write a general phrase that applies to the submission process: "Thank you for submitting your poetry to our publication. We appreciate your interest." Then follow up with a list of options, supplying a checkbox next to each so that the editor can simply "X" or check the most appropriate response. If you are most comfortable being conservative, offer the following options:

☐ We like your work and will contact you regarding publication.

☐ Your work has potential. Please send more samples.

☐ We cannot publish your poems at this time.

But if you feel like being gutsy, throw in one or two humorous (albeit unabashedly honest) options. Just make sure that you are willing to enjoy a laugh with the editors, instead of taking the response too seriously. The staff at Square One Publishers came up with these options. Warning: they get progressively brutal.

☐ You are no Walt Whitman (Anne Sexton, Langston Hughes, etc.), but you do have talent. Feel free to submit again, once you've begun writing *real* poetry.

☐ Perhaps we'll contact you for publication when we do an "April Fool's" edition.

☐ You're more likely to be picked up at a bar than picked up by a poetry publication. Get yourself a drink tonight!

☐ You seem to be ahead of your time. Get back to us when your time has come.

Keep in mind that some publications will be more appreciative of the humor than others. If you decide to create humorous postcards, use your professional sense to know where to send them.

cards, with prepaid postage, and including them in your submission packet. See "X Marks the Spot" above. A publication does not assume the responsibility of paying for the return of or response to unsolicited material.

Are you submitting to any international publications? If so, instead of including a standard SASE in the packet, purchase an IRC (International Response Card) at your local post office. An IRC is a type of receipt, confirming that you have paid a set amount of postage at your post office to cover the return mailing. The receiver can redeem the postage amount at *her* local post office. Ask your post-office official for help in determining how much postage you should purchase.

Proofread, Proofread, Proofread

Typos and grammatical errors are at the top of the list when it comes to "yucks" and "uh-oh's" from an editor's perspective. Taking the time to proofread your material is vital. Do not rely on your word processor's spell-check function; use your own two eyes. And if possible, also have a family member or friend glance over your work. You can get so used to your own stuff that you become blind to any mistakes.

While proofreading, do a simple check that the pages of your packet are clean—stain-free and rip-free. Let's face it, you'll probably have a cup of coffee next to you at some point; maybe even a sandwich. Also, be leery of unappealing details such as the lingering smell of cigarette smoke, or, quite differently, heavily perfumed paper. And when dealing with multiple pages and packages of material, things like paper clips and file organizers can bruise and tear paper. Be concerned with the appearance of the individual sheets in each submission package. Again, showing that you are serious and professional about your poetry endeavors will impress the editor.

Keep a Copy for Your File

Make a xerox copy or an extra print-out of each submission packet for your file. The other option is to keep copies of every-

> ### Helpful Hint
>
> It is important not to rely on computer spelling and grammar programs to catch typos and errors. Proofreading is absolutely necessary. Reread your poems and cover letters, and have a friend proofread them as well.

thing stored in your computer. Whatever the case, you'll have a way to confirm which poems went where. Plus, you'll have cover letters on hand to use as future guides. Finally, keeping a copy will save you a lot of time if you have to resend a package because the previous one was damaged in the mail or somehow misplaced (lost) by someone at the publication office.

Cleanly Label and Secure the Envelope

Choose a simple, sturdy envelope and seal it well. A business-sized, #10 envelope is suitable. If a magazine requires a large number of submissions and, thus, your submission package does not fit well within a regular envelope, a larger one is certainly acceptable. But keep in mind that the editor will be glad to receive a slim, well-organized packet whenever possible, so avoid adding extra size or bulk. Don't aim for fancy; aim for professional.

There's also a chance that the poetry or literary editor is not even opening the envelope. At larger publications, an assistant usually goes through the mail first and stacks your documents with other incoming mail, already opened for convenience, on the editor's desk. Staff members at publication offices complain about white envelopes marked up with such "senseless artistic efforts" as thick lines of green magic marker and childish stickers. A typical response is, "What am I—a kindergarten student? I don't need to be entertained by flashy colors and peel-off cartoon characters."

Do be sure that you label the mailing envelope, as well as your self-addressed and stamped envelope, clearly and cleanly. You may even want to type up a label, especially if your handwriting tends to be highly stylized. There's a place for calligraphy, such as on wedding invitations, but this is not one of them. Seal the package neatly and well; avoid ugly strips of tape or glue smears.

CONCLUSION

Feel confident that you know what to put in and what to leave out of your submission packages. You realize now that it is important to create cover letters that truly communicate your personality as a poet. You also understand the danger of going overboard with creative forget-me-nots on your poem print-outs, although a touch of creativity may distinguish you from the others. Always include a SASE and clearly label your envelopes. Once you've mastered the submission-package protocol, it's time to begin the Square One System for getting your poetry into print publication. You'll find this step-by-step plan in Chapter 5.

CHAPTER 5

---

*U*SING THE SQUARE ONE SYSTEM

I f you followed the guidelines in the last few chapters, you have already figured out a general marketing direction and you have familiarized yourself with a couple of market resources. Moreover, you know how to put together a great submission package. It's time to start using the Square One System, this chapter's seven-step strategy for getting into print. The Square One System will organize your submission process so that you can attain a suitable flow of submissions and responses. And while we're on the subject of sending your poetry out into the world, this chapter will also address such important issues as keeping a healthy perspective—everyone needs a little pep talk every now and then—and protecting your work.

THE SYSTEM

Achieving the print publication of poetry can be a frustrating thing. Why is it so hard these days? Because, as discussed in Chapter 1, while poetry is not a lucrative field, millions of people ache to share it. As a result, the market is flooded. The best way to handle these odds is to win your space through well-paced strategy. You need a mapped-out guide to follow, so that you don't end up overwhelmed and burned out by the whole process. The Square One System will help you find that happy medium between charging blindly into the attack and surrendering to the odds.

Please remember that this guide is geared toward the poet who is just starting to infiltrate the world of print. Therefore, the system offered in this chapter is shaped around submission to small literary magazines and journals.

Step One

The Square One System will help you find that happy medium between charging blindly into the attack and surrendering to the odds.

Your very first step is to prepare a long list of publications that are likely to publish your kind of poetry. Shoot for a roster of approximately twenty to thirty publications. The list should include the following information about each magazine: full name; address; phone and fax numbers; e-mail address and website address, if available; poetry editor's name and phone extension; circulation and press run information; and special notes on submission guidelines. Use the format arranged in the sample Tracking Chart on page 98, or create your own. The latter columns in the chart will be discussed shortly.

To find appropriate publications, use the resources discussed in Chapter 3. Some of these texts, such as *Poet's Market*, spell out most of the information for you, including submission guidelines and editors' names. Other resource books supply very limited information—publication names, general contact details, and some subject and circulation information. When using these latter sources, you will have to pursue guidelines concerning submission on your own, using whatever contact information you are given. Most editors prefer that you send a written request for guidelines, through the regular mail or e-mail, rather than phoning for details.

Do not underestimate the importance of obtaining and reading a submission guideline packet for each and every publication that you are considering. The packet reveals the editor's preferences for format, style, etc. If you ignore the special requests detailed in the packet, the editor will not look kindly upon you. Disregarding the editor's or publication's policies demonstrates a lack of respect and professionalism on the part of the poet.

You might have a tendency to limit yourself to one resource book that conveniently supplies a wealth of information. If this helps you to begin the process without overwhelming yourself, that's fine. But eventually work on expanding your resource library. You will outgrow even the bulkiest of resource books, so it's a good idea to familiarize yourself with more than one source. Also, the larger, well-known sources are used by most writers. Sometimes turning to a resource directory that is a little harder to get or a little more challenging to use might benefit you in the long run, as you pursue markets that others might not know about or bother with.

By the time you complete Step One, you should have all the important information necessary to submit to the publications of your choice. This information should be neatly arranged in your Tracking Chart (see sample on page 98). By this time, you should be able to fill in the first three columns. Storing the data in chart boxes makes the whole process cleaner and less intimidating; no flying index cards and piles of chicken-scratch notes for you!

Step Two

When prioritizing, there's nothing more effective than the "Top Ten" list—the best of the best. David Letterman has his top ten lists; Wayne and Garth have their top ten lists; now you will have your top ten list! Pulling from the twenty or more publications you chose during Step One, make a list of the ten publications that are most likely to publish your material.

Helpful Hint

Be sure to follow the detailed instructions in the submission guideline packets. In doing so, you demonstrate professionalism, respect, and serious interest.

TRACKING CHART

Name of Publication/ Editor/Contact Info	Guidelines	Circulation/ Press Run
1. *American Rhythms* Peter Marco, Poetry Ed. 1881 Lucia Street 10th Floor, Suite 1012 New York, NY 10021 Ph: 212-551-1222, ext. 342 Fx: 212-555-1122 E: Amrhy@bks.bks Web: http://www.amerhy@bks.bks/org	Ethnic/racial experiences, esp. musically influenced work; send 5–7 poems; all styles; looking for new writers	subscribers only; 500
2. *Poet's Pride* Jude Kastinski, Poetry Ed. 30 Chase Street Brimstone, ME 54321 Ph: 207-555-0000 Fx: 207-551-0000 E: poetry@ptry.ptry Web: http://www.poetpridemag.org	Transcendentalist works; 5 poems, 1 page each; new writers welcome * Accepts multiple submissions	Regional; 1,500

The sample tracking chart above shows how you can record all of the information relevant to each submission. This chart can be input on computer in landscape format, or written out on a regular 8.5 x 11-inch sheet of paper turned sideways, to maximize your writing space. You may also want to abbreviate the column headings in whichever way makes the most sense to you, so that you can fit them across the page.

Now that you've narrowed it down to a very manageable number, do some further research on these publications. Try to flip through issues at your public library, local university libraries, or nearby bookstores, including those online. Some publications send out a sample copy when you ask for submission guidelines, while others sell you one for a few dollars. The

Poems Sent	Response Time	Sent	Received	Response/ Date
"Little Brother's Taps" "New Waltz" "Bass In the Basement" "She Sang to Me" "The Moon Had Strings"	2–3 months	11/13/01	11/24/01	"New Waltz" accepted, 2/10/02
"My Own Eyes" "A Branded Brotherhood" "Down the Front Steps" "Far From Laurel"	6 weeks	11/15/01	11/22/01	Not interested, 12/28/02

more successful magazines and journals can be found at retail stores and libraries. In addition, stores in your town might carry regional publications.

If you are very serious about getting into print, you will research your selected magazines and journals well. Editors have noted that they are especially impressed when submitting authors are also readers of the publication. It softens an editor's heart when you mention an author whom his publication has introduced, or a specific issue that you truly enjoyed.

In gathering your full body of research, you may have a few dangling questions. Even though we are entering an "e-oriented" and "mail-me-the-request" world, there are times when you will have no other option than to use the phone. Maybe your mailed request went unanswered, or maybe the submission guidelines left something out. If you are phoning to gather more details about a small publication and there is no answer, don't get discouraged. The absence of a full-time assistant or multiple phone lines means this publication is quite small indeed. It may be in need of submissions! Just try again at a different time. If worse comes to worst, after several attempts to get hold of a staff member, send another note in the mail.

Step Three

Now we break it down even further. Prioritize your top ten choices. I'm talking about assigning an actual number to each entry. The "number one" publication should be the most promising or the one offering the best odds, and "number ten" on the list should be the least promising.

It is important to note that you should base your decision not only on the facts you see in your chart, but also on your own personal opinions and preferences. Your fondness for a publication's work is very likely to make a difference in your motivation to create a winning submission package. Your cover letter will be stronger and you will choose your submissions a little more carefully if you are preparing a package for a magazine you truly like. So if there is a publication that just catches your eye and gives you a good feeling, treat yourself and put it high on your list.

Step Four

Once you've prioritized the top ten, isolate the top five and get ready for work. Send a submission package to each of these publications. (See Chapter 4 for what to include in the submission packages, and for tips on how to make them both professional and creative.) Also, it's time to start filling in the later columns of the Tracking Chart on page 99. Record which poems were sent to each publication. Record the date that you send out each package. If you get a confirmation that the package was received, note the date on which you were alerted, as well. However, don't *expect* to be notified when your packet arrives. You could simply estimate the date of arrival and trust that it got there. Editors do not appreciate phone calls to confirm the receipt of submission packets.

Avoid the tendency to turn out five submission packages in one day, just so that you can feel like you are moving forward. If you can help it, don't let that sense of urgency get the best of you. Take the time to tailor each submission package to the specific publication. It is best not to view the submission process as a mass mailing. Getting an editor to consider your work is almost as much of an art as the actual writing of your poems. Be clever, take your time, and try to enjoy the process of discussing yourself and your work in each powerful little packet.

Step Five

Once the first five submission packages are in the mail, relax for eight weeks. This gives the various editors time to review your material and, hopefully, to respond. It also gives you time to step away, evaluate your work thus far, and recharge yourself. All you have to do during this step is keep track of any responses on your chart. That being said, it is true that some poets get on such a roll that they choose to continue researching more markets even during the waiting period. And, of course, keep working on your poetry—the actual *poems*. Remember them? There is a chance that some or all of the responses will come back within a shorter time than expected, such as within six weeks. If this occurs, move onto Step Six sooner.

In their submission guidelines, many publications list a time frame in which they will make a decision on your work. If this is the case with the publications to which you are submitting,

Are Multiple Submissions a No-No?

Multiple submission is a fancy label referring to when a writer submits the same piece of writing to more than one publication or publisher. *Simultaneous submission* is a synonymous term. Why would this be a problem? Well, what happens when more than one journal or magazine accepts the same poem for publication?

For the average writer, sending multiple submissions is a helpful practice. Several pairs of eyes will review the work, and hopefully one of them will like what they see. From the poet's point of view, getting into print is so challenging that the "multiple acceptances" problem is usually too remote to worry about.

However, multiple acceptances do happen. That's why many editors despise the practice of multiple submissions. An editor spends a lot of time selecting the most appropriate work. Usually, if the author can't deliver first serial rights (securing that the publication is the first to publish the work) after his piece has been accepted, the poem will have to be pulled out of production. Then the process begins again for the editor—hacking through the stacks of submissions, notifying the author of acceptance, sending the piece to typesetting and proofreading the results, etc. The sudden change in material could even cost the publication some money, depending on the stage at which it must be pulled. As a result of the trouble it can cause, some editors plead "No multiple submissions!" in their guidelines.

However, increasing numbers of literary editors are sympathizing with authors and accepting that multiple submissions are another part of modern-day publishing. For poets today, competition is fierce and reporting

Helpful Hint

Remember: During the "waiting periods," keep your poetry time slots reserved for doing additional research, reading, and writing.

make a note of the expected response times on your chart. Response times vary greatly. A good number of poetry publications respond within two to three months. However, there are those who promise answers within two to four weeks, and others who ask that you allow them six months. In short, consider the option of developing a pre-stamped, follow-up postcard that politely nudges the editor to respond. (See "'X' Marks the Spot" on page 90.)

Keep in mind that most publications receive more submissions than they can handle. It should not come as a surprise if a response is late. In addition, there may be situations in which times are painfully long. Is it really fair to expect a poet to keep five to six of his best poems in the drawer while a small magazine keeps the submission packet on the desk for two months? So there are plenty of editors out there who understand the necessity of multiple submissions. They do request a little courtesy, though. Amy Holman, in her article titled "Simultaneous Submissions: Yea or Nay?" gives some sound advice: "If you decide to simultaneously submit, first find out which magazines accept multiple submissions. . . . If you do simultaneously submit to magazines that allow the practice, without fail notify each editor in your cover letter." This way, the editor can't curse and blacklist you if you have to withdraw your poem after acceptance. Also, some editors try to review the work more quickly if they know it is being considered elsewhere.

Holman reminds us that accepted poems become occasions for "business deals." Publications compete with each other for the best new talent and the most promising pieces. Often, the publication's goal is to secure First North American Serial Rights, granting it the privilege of being the first to publish the work. Generally, after publication, rights go back to the author. Then he can include the poem in a collection, in an anthology, or in another publication that does not require first or sole rights.

If you don't alert an editor of multiple submissions in your cover letter and end up having to withdraw your poem, the editor is very likely to avoid reading work that you later submit. It is unwise to think that you are immune to this difficult situation. For information on how to handle multiple acceptances in a professional manner, see page 119.

you simply don't hear from the editor at a publication, even after a very generous wait. See "Send a Card" on page 104 for a good way to handle those long silences.

If and when you receive rejection letters, record these dates. Likewise, record the dates of any acceptances. There should be a final column in your chart for such very important pieces of information. Don't forget to record the name of the specific poem(s) accepted for publication. This way, you'll keep track of what is no longer "unpublished" work for the next time you submit. For more information on how to handle rejections, acceptances, and multiple acceptances, see Chapter 6.

Send a Card

After researching a publication, preparing a submission package designed specifically for that magazine, and mailing it out, it can be quite frustrating not to hear from the editor within the anticipated amount of time. What should you do with the long silences that leave you vulnerably lingering? Some of us are tempted to pick up the phone, brace our hearts, and ask the editor for an outright response. But follow-up calls will most likely frustrate and annoy the editor. He is bombarded with submission after submission, and is probably not going to remember yours by name, date, or subject matter. In fact, the editor may not even have gotten to your package yet, and will not appreciate a "hurry up and get to it" call.

So what can you do? Simply, send a card—not a Hallmark, but a follow-up postcard. The postcard should be self-addressed and its postage should be prepaid. On the card, type or print a message regarding the date that you mailed your submissions to the publication, and the fact that you have not received a response as of yet. Then, offer the editor an easy way out. That is, give the editor a list of optional responses, with checkboxes next to each one. It will only take a few seconds for him to read through the choices: "I read your submissions, but can't use them for this publication"; "I read your submissions and am presently considering your work"; "I have no record of receiving your submissions." He can simply check the one that is most appropriate.

Don't be afraid to be a little humorous or clever. The editor will probably appreciate it. On the next page is a sample postcard.

Step Six

It's time to take the next five entries from your top ten list. Repeat Steps Four and Five. That means preparing another five submission packages, mailing them out, and then keeping track of any responses that come in.

By now, you should be good at tinkering with and tailoring your cover letters and submission materials. The bigger worry is how to keep your motivation up. There's a chance that your first batch of submissions resulted in an acceptance, but there is a greater chance that you will have to reenact the Square One System several times before finding homes for your poems. Instead of getting down on yourself, take the whole thing on as a

> Dear Ms. Blake,
>
> My poetry submission package was mailed to your publication on November 15. As of yet, I have not obtained a response. I understand that you receive many submissions and do not have the time to prepare responses to all. I ask that you simply confirm the receipt and review of my work by checking one of the boxes below. Thank you.
>
> ☐ I received your submissions, but I didn't like them.
>
> ☐ I received and enjoyed your submissions, but I can't use them.
>
> ☐ I received and enjoyed your submissions, and I am considering them for publication.
>
> ☐ I did not receive your submission package. Please resend it.
>
> ☐ I don't remember receiving anything. Please leave me alone.

Obviously, the last option offers a touch of comedy. Who knows? The editor may take a second look at your work simply because you've demonstrated both wit and persistence. Editors appreciate the fact that a response postcard demands very little time and effort. The card can go into the mailbag after a simple check-off. However, out of courtesy to the editor's busy schedule, allow at least a month to pass before sending a response postcard.

challenge. See "Keeping Your Perspective" on page 106 for some words of encouragement.

Step Seven

Allow another eight weeks to pass by, always recording any feedback that you receive. Then, if you still have not received an acceptance, go back to that original list that you made during Step One. Choose the next ten entries and begin the process again. Start by further researching these publications as suggested in Step Two. If you have exhausted your original list, turn back to the resources and gather another twenty to thirty publication names. In this case, you'll be starting again at Step One.

KEEPING YOUR PERSPECTIVE

In order to maintain a healthy perspective, you must realize that it often takes many, many submissions before you have a poem accepted for print publication. Even the most established and respected poets have experienced multiple rejections. Perhaps these "songs of experience" will make you feel better.

Robert Frost

Robert Frost was born in San Francisco in 1874. Although he attended both Dartmouth and Harvard, he never earned a formal degree, and drifted through a string of jobs before becoming the most celebrated poet in America. While living in England from 1912 to 1915, Frost was influenced by many British poets, and established a friendship with Ezra Pound, who helped to promote and publish his work. The recipient of four Pulitzer Prizes, Frost lived and taught for many years in Massachusetts and Vermont, and died in Boston in 1963.

Who can argue the significance and influence of Robert Frost? He is an American voice in the most admirable sense of the phrase. Among his many accomplishments, Frost was a four-time Pulitzer Prize winner (1924, 1931, 1937, 1943) and the Poet Laureate of Vermont in 1961. (The *national* title of Poet Laureate was not yet in existence.) But Frost, like most poets, felt vulnerable when first submitting work. And he, like most poets, got rejected.

It is true that Frost's "My Butterfly" was the first poem he submitted for print and the first of his poems that went to print. In addition, "My Butterfly" was published in *The Independent*, a newspaper with national circulation. But *Robert Frost: Poetry and Prose*, edited by Edward Connery Lathem and Lawrance Thompson, exposes that prior to mailing a copy of "My Butterfly" to *The Independent's* editor, Reverend William Hayes Ward, Frost had received rejection slips. And in a letter to Ward, Frost honestly reveals, "The poem you have is the first of mine that any publication has accepted. At about the same time however that I sent you this, I disposed of three others in a similar way in other quarters. As yet they are not returned." Even the best have to wait, and even the best have to pay their dues.

In *Poetry and the Common Life*, M.L. Rosenthal writes, "[Frost] used his art to catch life on the run and then tried to hold the whole sense of it intact within a formal frame." You can apply Frost's approach to the submission process; carry out the process with energy and ambition, but use organized strategy and professionalism to frame your efforts.

Allen Ginsberg

Here's something you may not know about the celebrated Beat poet, Allen Ginsberg. According to *Journals: Early Fifties Early Sixties*, edited by Gordon Ball, Ginsberg was no stranger to feelings of frustration and disappointment. Ball reveals:

> . . . [Ginsberg's] *Empty Mirror*, with a preface ('the craft is flawless') by William Carlos Williams, had not found a publisher, while the manuscript of *The Gates of Wrath* was lost by a well-intentioned friend. . . . Thus while he thought of himself and Bill and Jack (and Gregory) [his writing companions] as literary souls already 'published in Heaven,' Ginsberg concluded after very futile efforts that little could be done in New York.

Even those who possess the greatest talent experience motivational slips and feelings of futility every once in a while. That's human. However, it's also human to get back up and try again. You might be headed for great places, and you don't want to let a setback get in your way.

Allen Ginsberg was born in Newark, New Jersey in 1926. While at Columbia University, he became close friends with Jack Kerouac and William Burroughs, who were later to be numbered among the Beats. In the early 1960s, Ginsberg began a life of ceaseless travel, reading his poetry at campuses and coffee bars, and engaging in left-wing political activities. Ginsberg is perhaps best known for his influence on the American youth counterculture in the late 1960s. He died in New York City in 1997.

A. R. Ammons

"Let-downs" happen to all kinds of poets, even those who charge ahead and aggressively publish full manuscripts. Many great poets, in desperate and unknown days, have published books that garnered no attention. For example, let's look at the early career of A.R. Ammons. He, too, is consistently included on the roster of best American poets. Ammons' long success list of published works might lead you to believe that he's been a winner from the get-go. But the truth is that Ammons' first

Archie Randolph Ammons was born in North Carolina in 1926, and started writing poetry aboard a U.S. Navy ship in the South Pacific. After World War II, Ammons attended Wake Forest University. Afterwards, he worked at a variety of jobs before he began teaching poetry at Cornell University in 1964. Ammons is the author of nearly thirty books of poetry, and has been awarded numerous prizes for his work, including the prestigious National Book Award.

From the
Poet's Pen

Author Marshall J. Cook wrote:

At first I resented time spent marketing. . . . But I learned to see it as an investment in my writing, as another set of skills to learn and a creative challenge to meet with energy and zest.

book of poetry, *Ommateum* (1955), was published by a vanity press, while Ammons worked at jobs not even remotely related to poetry.

No critics praised *Ommateum* because few people noticed it was there. Ammons was not familiar to any audience. Yet a decade later, when Ammons took a position as a faculty member at Cornell University, he began to be recognized as a powerful poet. Today, his list of awards and honors goes on and on, including two National Book Awards, the Frost Medal, the National Book Critics Circle Award, and a MacArthur Fellowship, just to name a few. Ammons' story illustrates that being a recognized poet takes patience and perseverance.

You probably are still muttering, "I'm a poet, not a marketing executive! I don't want to spend my days researching the details of tiny publications on the other side of the country, being confined by submission guidelines, and mailing packages at the post office." And that's understandable; for most of us, marketing is the dry side of being a poet. Yet well-researched, well-paced marketing of your poems will save you time and money in the long run. In his *Writer's Digest* article titled "10 Secrets of Getting Published," author Marshall J. Cook writes, "At first I resented time spent marketing. . . . But I learned to see is as an investment in my writing, as another set of skills to learn and a creative challenge to meet with energy and zest." That's great advice.

We can find good tips on keeping a healthy perspective in *Get Smart!: 365 Tips to Boost Your Entrepreneurial IQ.* In this text, Rieva Lesonsky has put together advice from some of the most successful entrepreneurs of our time. Among the wealth of hints, let's consider several pointers from Michael Jeffreys, concerning how to reach goals. (Michael Jeffreys wrote *Success Secrets of the Motivational Superstars.*) Jeffreys suggests "Do not be or act like a victim." This applies to those of us who begin to feel slighted and sorry for ourselves. We may feel like victims simply because we are artists who have been marred by the terrible world of business. We may even feel like poetry has lost its charm, now that it's become a product to sell. Jeffreys reminds us that we are in control of the situation. We're not wronged, we're just fighting for a chance like everyone else. Although they sometimes have their exclusive appeal, we have to drop the martyr complexes.

Next, Jeffreys reminds us to "[get] a purpose." You may say, "I have a purpose. I want my name in print." But if you can understand this whole marketing agenda in the context of a larger vision, you will actually learn to *like* the process. How? Well, renowned poet Stanley Kunitz brilliantly states that, for a poem to rise to its "complete fulfillment," an audience is necessary. You are allowing your poetry to come to fullest fruition by finding publications that bring it to the public. The marketing of your work is a necessary step in a beautiful endeavor. (For the record, Kunitz is the first American poet in the history of the United States to publish a new collection of poetry while in his nineties. Obviously, he's mastered the business of bringing his poetry to the masses.)

Number three on Jeffreys' list of success secrets is the willingness to pay the price. Just accept it; hard work and hard knocks are par for the course in order to reach admirable goals. You'll have to carve out your own niches. You'll have to start out small and build steadily. But in the end, it's worth it.

Jeffreys also advises us to remain focused. So even when we don't feel like spending hours looking through a couple of small literary magazines, we must keep to our convictions. It's not going to be any easier tomorrow. Finally, for a little inspiration, Jeffreys instructs the reader to "be a copycat." For the poet, that means reading about other poets' careers, how others made it in the tough world of print publication. Imitate their gumption and follow their pointers. And speaking of copycats, if you are concerned about the safety of your poems in the hands of many, read the next section on protecting your work.

From the Poet's Pen

William Wordsworth, in his "Preface to the Lyrical Ballads" (1805 version), labeled the works of some contemporary poets as useless verse. He then wrote:

From such verses the poems in [my] volumes will be found distinguished by at least one mark of difference, that each of them has a worthy purpose.

A strong sense of purpose is essential to the role of the poet, whether in the creative process or the submission process.

HOW DO I PROTECT MY WORK?

Fear of having your work stolen is largely unnecessary, but completely natural. For peace of mind, do any one (or more) of the following: register the work with the United States Copyright Office (which takes approximately eight months for completion); obtain a notary public's stamp on an original document; establish a common copyright through standard notation on an original document; or mail yourself a copy of the work and keep it sealed.

As we discuss sending so many poems out to so many people, you may begin to feel a twinge of panic: "Am I losing control of my own work? Will someone copy it?" If you start to get a little overprotective, you're not alone. The fear that someone, somewhere, will steal or modify the work is a common concern for the writer who is just starting to submit literature for publication.

However, it is important to understand that, for the most part, this fear is unnecessary. Legal battles launched against copycat poets are terribly few, if not nonexistent. Usually, the sharing that occurs within the poetry community is good-spirited. Perhaps a fellow poet will become inspired by a particular work or style and will be influenced by it. Such a circumstance is flattering to the poet, not criminal. And most often, poets are very good about acknowledging their mentors.

For a wider perspective, let's look more deeply into the role of the poet. A poet displays original poetry in the hope that it changes the reader's outlook just a little, or that the reader finds consolation and community through the words. People drawn toward the art of poetry are motivated by a desire to create and effect change. Poetry is not a lucrative business; it's one of expression and service. As a result, there are very few thieves within the community. And someone would have to be pretty delusional to believe that stealing a few poems would result in financial benefit or world fame. Therefore, allow yourself to let go of consuming fears that the sin of plagiarism will be committed against you.

Notice that I recommend letting go of "consuming fears." Paralyzing fears are unnecessary. That being said, it is not *unreasonable* to take precaution, if you feel inclined to do so. There is nothing wrong with securing a copy of your work under your own name. It will give you peace of mind and a significant legal edge if, by some stroke of rare and bad fate, you happen to be wronged by a poetry pilferer. So, you ask, "What's the best way to protect my work?"

There is actually built-in protection, simply established through a hard copy of your creation. A *copyright* is yours as soon as you put your work down on a piece of paper or in a recording. Copyright is defined as the legal right to exclusively control the publication, production, and sales of a creative work. It offers legal protection from unauthorized copying or use of the work. Unless you agree to put your work's copyright under another name, you have the say when it comes to printing and reprinting.

To protect your work further, though, seek a visual representation of copyright for your own records. There are four ways to do this: registering the copyright with the United States Copyright Office; obtaining a notary public's stamp; establishing a common copyright through a standard notation on copies you simply hand out for review among peers; or sending a completed and signed copy of your work to yourself in the mail. Each of these procedures is discussed in more detail below.

The United States Copyright Office, located in Washington, D.C., is a part of the Library of Congress. There is a fee involved in registering your work with this office, but peace of mind and certain proactive legal benefits make it worth the time and money for some writers.

First, there is one *very* important point to make: *do not submit poetry with copyright notification to editors. Furthermore, do not call an editor and ask how you can protect your work from being stolen before you submit it.* Such practices are insulting to the editor; you give the impression that you don't trust his integrity, and you also demonstrate a lack of experience and professionalism. Keep copies that contain copyright information for your own records, but don't send these sheets out for submission.

Registering Copyright With the Federal Government

The United States' federal government has a copyright office with which you can register your copyright for a fee. The registration gives you certain legal benefits. Both unpublished and published work can be registered, and you do not have to re-

register a work if its status moves from the former to the latter (though you can register such material as another edition, if you wish). The United States Copyright Office, which is part of the Library of Congress, confirms that registration is not necessary for copyright privileges to be instituted. However, there are certain benefits to registering with the federal office.

Through registration with the United States Copyright Office, you have what is referred to as a "public record of the basic facts of a particular copyright." This gives you a legal edge; it's additional public proof that the work is your own. Also, if a writer feels his copyright has been violated, that writer will need to be registered with the federal copyright office (for works written with the United States) before legal action can take place. So, rare as it is, if you face a legal battle over copyright issues, already being registered within the United States Copyright Office will speed up the process and avoid complications.

Here are some other legal details. If copyright is registered with this office either before or within five years from the publication date, the registration will serve as "prima facie evidence." That means that, in a court of law, your registration certificate will most likely serve as sufficient evidence. And if you register your work with the copyright office within three months of its appearance in public print or before any violation of your rights has occurred, you will be awarded the money to pay for attorney expenses, as well as compensation for the wrongs committed against you, in the case that you do have to battle it out with a copyright infringer. Registration with the United States Copyright Office also makes available ways to protect your work from being imported from outside countries in any unethical or abusive manner.

If you decide that a federal copyright registration is for you, it is possible to register the work at any time. In other words, you can register a poem that you wrote thirty years ago, without any problem. As mentioned before, there is a fee involved, and a standard application protocol. First, you have to obtain an application form. There are several ways to get one: you can download the form from the Internet or request that one be mailed to you. Contact information for the United States Copyright Office is listed on page 165. Once you fill out the form, mail it to the office, along with the filing fee and a copy of the work you are registering. The fee is not refundable, and the copy is not returnable. If you don't hear from the copyright office within a few days, don't worry. It actually takes about eight months for copyright registration to go through! You will not be notified when your package reaches the office, but you will be mailed a certificate of registration once your application has been reviewed and accepted.

Contact information for the United States Copyright Office is listed on page 165.

Obtaining a Notary Public's Stamp

A notary public is, among other things, a person who has been officially authorized to certify or witness the placing of a signature on a document, to confirm that the paper has been signed on a given date. Each notary public has an exclusive ink stamp, containing his identification number. If you don't know one yourself, there are many places where you can find a notary public, including banks, financial offices, and many professional offices. Before releasing a given work, to establish visual proof of possession, you can bring a copy to a notary public and sign it in his presence. Then, the notary public will stamp, sign, and date the document. This will serve as legal proof that the writing was in your possession at the recorded date.

Establishing a Common Copyright Through Standard Notation

As explained earlier, copyright is established as soon as you write down or record your work. So you can simply place a copyright notation on the document containing that work. This

Helpful Hint

Don't fret if you don't hear from the United States Copyright Office within a few days. The review and acceptance of material can actually take about eight months.

Helpful Hint

Remember: do not include copyright notations on the pages of your submission packet. Such notations imply a distrust of the publication staff and might insult the editor.

is referred to as a *common copyright.* It is simply a visual reminder that you have the rights to that piece of literature. The United States Copyright Office suggests the following format to express copyright: The copyright symbol (©), followed by the year and your name. For example, in the footer (lower margin) of each of his works, William Shakespeare could have inserted: © 1591 William Shakespeare. Common copyright notation can be used whether or not you register with the United States Copyright Office. Another standard format, used by most professionals in the publishing industry, is: Copyright © 1591 William Shakespeare.

Inserting a common copyright on pages that you hand around for review to peers, etc., may put your mind at ease. You can combine a common copyright with any of the other methods for securing public knowledge of your copyright. But remember, don't put such a notation on copies you submit to editors.

Mailing Yourself a Copy of Your Work

Instead of paying the fee and filling out the forms for a federally registered copyright, some writers mail a completed and signed copy of their work to themselves. To use their technique, first add your signature and the date to the bottom of the document (or manuscript), seal it securely in an envelope, and address the envelope to yourself. Then take the packet to the post office and ask the person at the desk to hand-stamp each seam of the envelope with an official *dated* post office stamp. The packet will find its way back to your mailbox (or local post office for pick-up), complete with the post office's stamp telling what date and at what location the envelope was sent to its destination. It will also bear the stamped envelope seams, which will prove that you did not tamper with the package after receiving it in the mail. If left sealed, this document can serve as visual evidence that the piece of writing was complete and in your possession prior to the postal-stamp date.

Want to go a step further? Send your package via certified mail. It's more expensive, but then you will have additional proof that the work has been yours since a specific date. The package will be given a tracking number and logged in the mailing service's system. No one can argue with that.

If you feel a little nervous about sending your "children"—your poems, that is—out into the world, know that you are normal. With time, the whole process will become more comfortable and you will become less concerned with abuses such as thievery. But also understand that you are not paranoid if you decide to seek an official recognition of copyright. Such action affords many writers peace of mind. Again, none of the above-described methods are required for establishing copyright—it is yours as soon as you fix your work on paper or tape. However, a formally recognized copyright is a good security measure for those who tend to worry about protecting their work.

The process of sending your poems out for review will become less nerve-wracking with time. You will find yourself worrying less and less about abuses such as plagiarism.

CONCLUSION

The Square One System serves as a guide to help you stay organized and to carry out your endeavors at a reasonable pace. If you faithfully follow the system detailed in this chapter, your chances for publication will be much increased. Hopefully, you have also found some helpful tips on perspective in this chapter. Maintaining motivation can be challenging, but the rewards are great.

As you carry out the Square One System, responses to your submissions will arrive in the mail. The next chapter tells you how to evaluate and handle the results of your submission process, and also suggests alternatives if you find yourself hitting a brick wall after truly thorough efforts.

CHAPTER 6

$\mathcal{E}$VALUATING THE RESULTS

Sooner or later, those response notes are going to start coming in the mail. When they do, despite weeks of anxious waiting, you might want to stop time. Go ahead, open them up. You will have what it takes to respond well to anything those envelopes contain because this chapter will have prepared you for handling whatever results may come.

There are three scenarios to consider. First, you might have a poem accepted for print. Furthermore, if you've been carrying out the practice of multiple submissions, you might have to deal with multiple acceptances. Then there's the least desirable scenario: your poems are rejected for print. Each of these situations is discussed below. And just in case the rejection slips consistently bombard your mailbox, even after you put your best efforts forward and truly exhaust the marketplace, this chapter offers a number of other options to consider.

WHAT TO DO IF YOU RECEIVE AN ACCEPTANCE

Congratulations! Your efforts paid off and now you will see your

Helpful Hint

In the excitement of an acceptance, don't forget to update your submission chart and to add your success to your cover letter file. Don't abandon the system!

own name in print. You can feel confident that others recognize your talent, and moreover, that others will now hear your voice. You are taking an active part in the writers' community—a community that effects change and strives for movement. Be proud of yourself.

After celebrating your accomplishment, don't forget about the practical side. Go back to that Tracking Chart discussed in Chapter 5. Fill in the date on which you received the acceptance, and list the name(s) of the work(s) to be published. Add your success to your cover letter file as well; you will want to include information on this acceptance in your next cover letter.

Some acceptance letters contain details about publication, payment, etc., while others simply alert you to your success. In the case of the latter, a phone call or a more detailed letter will follow. Some writers report that they were surprised at how understated the whole process is. After all, upon the first few acceptances, a poet is beside himself with pride and joy. Although notification is quiet, an acceptance is an acceptance, and you'll love it even if there are no helium balloons tucked into the envelope.

Receiving an acceptance letter is a sure way to gain in confidence. That can make a real difference in your energy level and your writing, especially when producing new cover letters and motivating yourself to start new poems. But also realize that there is a good chance that the struggle for print publication will continue to be a struggle. Even the most promising poets continue to deal with rejections. So enjoy the feeling, but maintain perspective.

Now is also the time to take a really good look at the process that got you into print. Notice what type of publication selected you. Reread the cover letter that you composed for the specific editor. Observe how your accepted poem relates to the target audience. In other words, take note of what you did especially well. Finally, take advantage of the "in" that you now have at this magazine or journal. The editor likes you, and he is likely to be interested in considering more of your poetry for future issues. So go ahead and make the most of it—send another batch!

WHAT TO DO IF YOU RECEIVE MULTIPLE ACCEPTANCES

We discussed the issue of multiple submissions in Chapter 5. The practice used to be terribly frowned upon. However, publishers of poetry, in particular, are realizing that it is unfair to tie up numerous poems for long periods of time. So the practice of multiple submissions, also called simultaneous submissions, is becoming more accepted. This means that the situation of multiple acceptances is also becoming more common.

> **Helpful Hint**
>
> Out of courtesy for the publication from which you must withdraw, alert the editor of your withdrawal as soon as possible. The longer you wait, the more difficult it will be for the editor to make necessary adjustments.

If your poem is accepted by more than one publication, go back and look at your notes on each magazine. Did the editor express that simultaneous submissions are acceptable? Did he or she specifically request, "No multiple submissions!" but you went ahead and tempted fate anyway? First, find out where you stand. You may strike it lucky and realize that the magazines do not require first rights. If they are open to both unpublished and published work, they shouldn't have a problem with a multiple acceptance. But most small magazines and literary journals do want to showcase never-before-seen work. So chances are you'll have to make a decision and choose one publication (unless one of the magazines is published overseas, in which case there is no contest for First North American Serial Rights).

Some writers necessarily end up withdrawing from the publications that respond later, because they've already gone into contract with the first magazine to respond. However, if timing is good, you may have the luxury of choosing which publication to accept. If you find yourself in this dilemma, go with your preference. Of course, the larger-circulation or more renowned magazine is the likely choice. But if both magazines are similar in recognition and circulation, allow yourself to be guided by personal taste. Then start drafting your letter(s) of withdrawal to the "losing" publication(s). You really should inform editors of your withdrawals as soon as possible, out of courtesy.

A letter of withdrawal should contain a sincere and professional apology. The following letter serves as an example:

Sample Letter of Withdrawal

(Current Date)

Lynne Fagan, Poetry Editor
Muse and Meaning
4567 Cairo Avenue
Juno, VT 54321

Dear Ms. Fagan,

While I am truly honored to learn that you have accepted my poem, "New Waltz," for print, I regret to inform you that I must withdraw my work. Due to other obligations, this poem cannot be printed in your publication. However, I am enclosing another poem, similarly crafted, for your review. I apologize for this terrible inconvenience and hope that you find this latest submission comparable. Please let me know if there is anything further I can do to resolve this situation.

My sincere apologies,

Felicia Bonina
789 Terrace Boulevard
Hatfield, KS 23456
Phone: 789–123–4567
E-mail: febo@write.us

Sometimes you will come into contact with an angry editor. But that should only occur if the publication specifically demands no simultaneous submissions in its guidelines. In such a case, you have disrespected a request, so the editor may feel very justified in clearly stating that your work is no longer welcome at the publication. If this happens, learn from the situation, forgive yourself, and move on.

WHAT TO DO IF YOU ARE REJECTED

A rejection notice doesn't come with a skull-and-crossbones stamp. You won't find "LOSER" in red ink across the envelope. You will simply receive the SASE that you included in your submission package, containing a (usually) printed rejection slip or card that contains one of countless ways to state "submissions rejected." (See the inset "Should I Expect Feedback From Publications That Reject me?"on page 125). Suffice it to say that a rejection letter is quick and clear. Now what do you do? First, let's talk about how to view rejections from editors. Then we'll discuss what to do if you come to a disturbing conclusion: "The problems are within my poems, not the editors' personal opinions."

Neither a Permanent Stain
Nor a Personal Attack

The Writer's Handbook includes "A Guide to Dealing with Rejection," an essay by writer Fred Hunter. Hunter reminds us that editors are people just like you and me; they are people with personal tastes and preferences. Hunter is confident that editors do rise above their personal tastes and they do review the submissions with objective standards in mind. However, Hunter also remarks that, in the end, editors are no more likely to select a work that just doesn't appeal to them than you or I are likely

Having poems rejected is not a permanent mark that will prevent you from becoming a respected poet. Every poet suffers publication rejection.

to choose to read poems that we don't like. It is easy to understand how, on a subconscious level, personal preferences affect professional decisions.

You should not take each and every editor's opinion as though it were gospel. In fact, many writers who have received comments from editors claim that they have been given contradictory feedback. One editor might find the imagery effective but dislike the line breaks, while another might comment on inconsistent imagery but find the line breaks creative. That's not to say that editors are unskilled or that you should ignore their comments. On the contrary, if you do get feedback—which is rare—seriously consider it. But also realize that it is coming from a human being who feels pulled toward certain works and away from others. Don't allow your confidence to be terribly shaken by a rejection letter.

The constant deluge of poetry submissions is bound to put a strain on editors, encouraging haste and frustration. As a result, editors aren't always reading with open minds, nor are they often willing to give second readings, which some works require for true appreciation. In "How to Read Rejection," printed in a recent issue of *Poets & Writers*, editor C. Michael Curtis of the

---

Rejected, Not Dejected

✖ ✖ *C. Michael Curtis, in his article titled, "How to Read Rejection" advises, ". . .a writer ought to fight back the impulse to read rejection as a repudiation, a sign of hostility, or proof of ineptitude." Put simply, rejection should not cause dejection. Sure, you will feel disappointed. However, remember your initial reason for writing poetry—your passion. Don't let go of that passion so easily. It's one thing to be turned down for publication. It's another to turn against yourself by giving up.* ✖ ✖

Helpful Hint

Atlantic Monthly remarks, "Every magazine, no matter how rigorous in its screening and selection of candidates for publication, has a history of writers misjudged, talent unappreciated, opportunities for discovery overlooked."

Take the example of Emily Dickinson's review by a literary critic, mentioned briefly in the "Introduction." The story starts back in 1862. Thomas Wentworth Higginson authored a major article in the magazine *Atlantic Monthly*. It was titled "Letter to a Young Contributor" and offered practical advice on getting published. At the time, Emily Dickinson was thirty-one years old and ready for some professional critical review. She sent a letter in April of that year, asking Higginson to tell her if her poetry "breathed." Dickinson was confident in doing so because Higginson was particularly interested in women writers and their issues. But the critic did not find Dickinson's verses to be publishable! Although impressed by the poetry, its style and form were so unfamiliar that Higginson privately questioned whether it was poetry at all.

At least Higginson did ask for more of Dickinson's writing, as well as information on her age, reading, and companionship. Thus began a long correspondence that heavily influenced Dickinson's opinion of her own writing purposes. By her third letter to Higginson, Dickinson's decision not to be published during her lifetime was evident. She wrote, "I smile when you suggest that I delay 'to publish'—that being foreign to my thought as Firmament to Fin. . . . My Barefoot Rank is better." We can only wonder at what would have happened if she followed the Square One System!

Fred Hunter, mentioned earlier, also wisely suggests that we continue to work on other pieces of writing as we receive rejections from publishers. Keep your creativity well oiled; keep honing your skills. Hunter gives the example of Madeleine L'Engle, a celebrated author of both fiction and nonfiction. L'Engle was successful when it came to getting several novels published early in her career. However, she went through a

From the Poet's Pen

In the face of rejection slips and acceptance letters, keep writing! *Robert Frost: Poetry and Prose* contains a section titled, "Poetry and School: Remarks From His Notebooks." In his school notes, Frost confirms the unparalleled importance of actually writing, as opposed to merely discoursing on it:

Practice of an art is more salutary than talk about it. There is nothing more composing than composition.

Rejection notices are as understated as acceptance letters. They are plain and brief. And once you get used to the process, they become less painful.

ten-year dry spell during which she did not receive any acceptances. L'Engle, in her book titled *A Circle of Quiet,* explains that she didn't stop writing even during that discouraging period. She further developed her skills and eventually won the Newbery Medal for *A Wrinkle in Time.*

No one in the poetry circuit is ever going to write an article on all of your rejection letters and leave it at that. Having your poems declined for print is not a permanent mark that will prevent you from becoming a respected poet. Writers have their works rejected as often as shoes get marred with water, mud, and snow. That doesn't mean the pair of shoes is inadequate; it means the weather was nasty that day.

In the *Writer's Digest* article "Rejection Won't Kill You," author Suzanne Falter-Barnes offers words of wisdom. After unsuccessfully trying to find a publisher for her first novel through her own efforts and those of a literary agent, Falter-Barnes writes, "Immediately, I began to understand something about rejection: It's nothing personal." She realized that none of the editors was attacking who she is or what she stands for. They were not insulting her way of life or her intelligence. Therefore, she states that she learned "nonattachment," which involves realizing that her identity as a human being is not determined by the pieces of literature that she creates.

Falter-Barnes' article concludes with a comforting sentiment: what's most important at the end of the day is that you have tried to move a little closer to your dream. As long as you feel that you made your best effort, you've been successful. And Fred Hunter's essay, discussed earlier, closes with a quote from Disraeli: "The secret of success is constancy of purpose." So keep trying!

Perhaps a Valid Reason Why

Writers have their works rejected as often as shoes get marred with water, mud, and snow. That doesn't mean the pair of shoes is inadequate; it means the weather was nasty that day.

The poetry world is flooded and even great poetry gets turned away. Sometimes you can simply chalk it up to bad luck or

Should I Expect Feedback From Publications That Reject Me?

Considering all the work that you've put into each submission packet, it would be nice if the editors could at least write a few comments, whether in the form of encouragement or constructive criticism. But the reality is that very few editors have the time to make handwritten notes offering advice. When submissions first arrive, an assistant or the editor herself stacks the packages on the desk. This pile is endearingly termed the *slush pile* throughout the industry. The editor looks helplessly at the amount of work, and then begins several long hours of quick decisions. If your work catches the editor's eye, it will make it to the next cut, but if it's not what the editor is hoping for, a quick rejection is in order.

Thus, do not expect to get feedback from the editors. Once in a while, if a poem makes it to the top tiers of selection, you may receive a note with some encouragement or criticism. However, this is *very* rare. So it is smart to familiarize yourself with a local group of writers whom you respect. They can be your support system and your critics. If you gather together an honest and articulate bunch, you can rely on them for in-depth reviews of your work.

inconvenient timing. But there also may be an identifiable reason why you are receiving rejection slips consistently. It's good to check yourself by considering a couple of possibilities. Are you: targeting the wrong publications?; presenting your materials ineffectively?; lacking necessary quality in your work or choosing the wrong poems?

First, take a second and third look at the types of publications to which you are submitting. Maybe there are niches that you haven't even considered or didn't know about. Discuss your endeavors with fellow writers, at online forums, at poetry readings, etc. By talking to other poets and writers, you may get some new ideas concerning where to submit your poetry. Second, have several people review some samples of the submission packages you are sending out. (Remember, you should

If your short-term goals have not been met after a long time, consider why. Are you targeting the wrong audience? Presenting your work ineffectively? Submitting poems that are underdeveloped and/or lack the necessary quality?

keep a copy of everything. Copies will come in handy when seeking peer reviews.) Perhaps you are a great poet, but not such a great letter writer. Or maybe you've gone a little overboard when trying to be creative with your package. Feedback from peer reviews might clue you in to your weaknesses.

If you've still come up with nothing, try turning to your actual poems. This is the most painful part. You may have to come to terms with the fact that your craft is not yet fully developed. If this is the case, there are several things you can do.

Read, Write, and Listen

Nothing can replace reading as a method for skill enhancement. Read guides on the craft of poetry, such as those recommended in the Resource Directory. In doing so, you'll pick up clues on how to become a more effective poet. Also, read plenty of poetry books. They will exercise your imagination, influence your style, and develop your poetic ear—which ultimately leads to the maturation of your poetic voice. In his article titled "10 Secrets of Getting Published," Marshall J. Cook reminds us to read not only well-written material, but also the not-so-good stuff. Reading mediocre and poorly constructed poetry gives you the opportunity to read critically. You will start to identify what makes these poems uncomfortable on your tongue, in your ear, and on the page. Then, you can apply the study to your own work.

In addition, read all sorts of poetry, not just the kind that parallels your own style and interests. Get a feel for various styles, rhythms, and voices. Exposing yourself to different types of poetry may trigger big changes in your own writing. You might find a new rhythm or form that works well with your skills.

While you are reading and reading, remember to maintain your writing machine. You might have allowed the publication process to stunt you. Did you become obsessed with the marketing of your poems and end up miles away from your craft?

Well, return to the basics—the creation and articulation of verse. Don't stop writing, even if you simply scrawl a few thoughts down on paper in the evening. As you increase your reading, your style and level of writing is very likely to change.

Also, attend poetry readings and listen carefully. Developing your listener's ear will make you a better reader and writer. You'll learn how to effectively use such techniques as alliteration and onomatopoeia. Your appreciation for pause and rhythm will increase. Finally, you'll learn how to perform poetry, in case you decide to present your work to an audience.

Three-time Poet Laureate Robert Pinsky confirms that readers should be listeners too. He tells us to read poetry aloud in order to grasp its full effect. Reading your own poems aloud, even just to yourself, allows such weaknesses as rhythm breaks and awkward phrasing to become more apparent.

By reading, writing, and listening more, your skills as a poet are very likely to improve. It may sound time consuming, but it doesn't have to be. Just give whatever time you can—even brief snippets of writing and reading time at the end of the day or during your lunch hour. Thus, your creativity and progress will continue to develop, like an exercised muscle.

Get Involved With a Writers' Group

Writers benefit from taking part in a group of similarly motivated and creative people. Therefore, if you don't already belong to one, consider joining a writers' group. In such a setting, you will have the opportunity to enhance your writing with the support of people who appreciate your passions, tensions, and dreams.

"How do I become a member?" you ask. Raymond Obstfeld gives great advice in his article, "How to Make Your Writers' Group Better," published in *Writer's Digest*. First, you could start your own group. This allows you the benefit of picking and choosing the starting members. If you are attending a writing class, regular poetry readings, lectures, etc., talk to the writers

From the Poet's Pen

Robert Pinsky's "Library Scene," describes the intensity of the person who reads with curiosity:

Someone is reading,
in the sleepy room
Alert, her damp cheek
balanced on one palm,

With knuckles loosely
holding back the pages
Or fingers waiting lightly
at their edges.

Her eyes are like the eyes
of someone attending
To a fragile work, familiar
and demanding—

around you and get to know their approaches and interests. Match yourself with people who have similar goals and can articulate well. Then suggest meeting at a local coffee shop—or at your place, if you know the writers well enough to trust them. Tell them that you are trying to form a writers' group that will meet once every two weeks, or once a month (whatever your schedules allow), to share writings, tips, and encouragement. You might be very pleasantly surprised at the results. Aim to gather only four or five members. That way, everyone will have the chance to share and comment.

In order for a writers' group to be productive, the members have to get along well, trust each other, care about each other, and be compatible in intelligence and focus. The members should be at approximately the same point in their writing careers, as well.

Another option is to check for advertisements in local newspapers, flyers, school bulletins, coffee-shop and library posting boards, etc., for groups that are in the midst of being formed or that are looking to fill a chair. Certainly allow yourself to be picky, whether you are joining a group or selecting a member for your own. In order for a writers' group to be productive, the members have to get along well, trust each other, care about each other, and be compatible in intelligence and focus. The members should be at approximately the same point in their writing careers.

Yet another option is to join an online writers' group. Many groups are available, as well as open forums and chat rooms. But a solid, committed group is best. Online writers' groups do not foster the camaraderie and trust that "in-person" groups do. But if you cannot commit to physically meeting with a group, online groups are better than nothing. Actually, there is a plus to them: if you don't like the group, it's very easy to leave. Nobody will be relying on you for meeting space or for your compassionate looks across the table.

Writers' groups aren't always wonderful experiences, and if you find that yours is not up to par, find or start another one. It is better to leave or disband than to allow the group to become destructive to the individual writers. Participants might not get along; the pace of the group might frustrate some members; perhaps several participants approach the group as a social event instead of an educational process. If it's not working for you, as hard as it may be, move on.

In his article, discussed earlier, Obstfeld offers further pointers for a successful writers' group. Definitely establish a scheduled meeting time and the need for regular attendance. If members stick to a time slot and the promise to produce work for it, motivation and productivity will blossom. Obstfeld also suggests carefully assessing a prospective member before signing her into the group. Have the person attend a meeting. Observe her articulation skills, concentration, manner, and feedback techniques. Finally, Obstfeld recommends that members read the discussion material prior to the meeting. This is a great suggestion, so that everyone has time to organize thoughts, take notes, and prepare good responses.

For poets, it is important to encourage reading aloud during the meetings, as well as beforehand. In fact, one great option is to have members read other members' work. We get so used to our own work that we cannot approach it objectively. Hearing our own poems read at different paces than we prescribe or with different pauses than we expect will help us be more critical and objective.

Bear in mind, though, that it is not always easy for the poet to hear her own work read aloud, especially if she is not fond of the reader's interpretation. During such times, the poet must exercise self-control, avoid interrupting, and do her best not to become emotionally reactive. So if you find yourself in this situation, and feel yourself breaking into a sweat, make a conscious effort to temporarily disown the poem. Simply pretend that you are just another listener. It will become easier with practice.

Consider Some Professional Training

There are countless training programs available to poets. Some are informal, like local workshops. Others are annual writers' conferences. Then there are writing classes at local schools. Or, if you have the money, skill, and educational background, there are degrees in writing and literature that you could pursue to hone your skills.

If you are looking for a local workshop, contact your local and state arts councils. Furthermore, you can find out about programs from your Town Hall, regional magazines and newspapers, at your library, through schools, etc. For example, YMCAs across the country sponsor YMCA National Writer's Voice Centers. Many different writers' events take place at these community centers, from poetry readings, to workshops, to writing camps, to school residencies.

Poets' and writers' organizations are great sources of information on upcoming events and programs. Call the organizations, such as the ones listed in the Resource Directory beginning on page 147, for their calendars of events. They may be sponsoring a lecture series in your region, or offering a summer workshop that you can attend. Request that you be notified about upcoming events via e-mail or standard mail.

Also, check out the ads in magazines such as *Poets & Writers, Writer's Digest, The Writer,* and *Writers' Journal.* You'll find information on well-respected programs that vary in length from one-day workshops to weekend seminars to several-month writing retreats. In addition, consult the market resources named in Chapter 3. Many of these sources (such as *Poet's Market*) offer good summaries of numerous conferences and workshops, listing everything from price to level of writer desired. Some conferences are rather expensive and exclusive, but many welcome the general public. The costs for conferences can vary greatly, from under $100 for a three-day seminar to over $1,000 for a conference that lasts two weeks or more. Prices change from year to year, however, so contact the organization to get exact prices. And be sure to investigate the programs fully. Here's a brief example of the varied choices you'll find.

In the *Poet's Market's* "Conferences & Workshops" section, you'll find the Sewanee Writers' Conference listed. This is a twelve-day annual event that attracts over 100 participants. Poets, playwrights, and fiction writers attend. However, participants are selected after submitting full manuscripts for review; this program is not open to the public. In late July, the participants reside at The University of the South Campus, in Sewanee, Tennessee, where all classes and events take place. Some scholarships and fellowships are available, awarded on merit.

A very different type of conference is the Tennessee Mountain Writers Conference in Oak Ridge, Tennessee. This is a yearly, three-and-a-half day event that takes place in the springtime and is hosted at a hotel. The conference is open to all levels and types of writers—"all aspiring writers, including students." There are speakers, contests, and a book fair that promotes the participants' books. Attendees are asked to submit ten pages of work prior to the conference, so that individual critiques are possible.

A final example is the UND Writers Conference, taking place at the University of North Dakota's campus in Grand Forks. This four- to five-day, late-winter event gathers several thousand people over the course of the conference! There is no fee for the events, and writers at all levels are encouraged to attend. The goal is public education. Recognized poets take part in readings, panel discussions, dinners, receptions, etc. There are open-mike readings and informal discussions, as well.

It is evident that there are all sorts of conferences to choose from, and all sorts of levels of participation. Some are geared toward a select group of serious, professional writers, while others promote public education and invite all to attend. You are sure to find several that catch your eye. When you do, write to the contact person for brochures, an application, and other registration material, and don't forget your SASE.

As mentioned previously, there are a number of academic degrees that can enhance your skills as a writer. Master degrees in the fine arts (MFAs), creative writing, and literature, for example, are wonderful ways to get you started on a serious poetry career. But reputable institutes—a few of which are Bread Loaf,

Gwendolyn Brooks was born in Topeka, Kansas in 1917, and was raised in Chicago. She is the author of more than twenty books of poetry. In 1968, Brooks was named Poet Laureate for the state of Illinois, and from 1985 to 1986, she was Consultant in Poetry to the Library of Congress. She has received an American Academy of Arts and Letters award, the Pulitzer Prize, the Frost Medal, fellowships from The Academy of American Poets and the Guggenheim Foundation, a National Endowment for the Arts award, and the Shelley Memorial Award.

Sewanee, Stanford, and Johns Hopkins—usually choose applicants who are mid-career, so to speak. The students have already demonstrated serious commitment and tremendous skill, evidenced through recommendations, carefully evaluated writing samples, fellowships from various sponsors, and previous academic endeavors. As for the cost, many students are awarded grants, tuition wavers, and the like to help them out. But this option is for the person who can afford both the time and money involved with being a serious student.

Attending workshops and conferences can truly make a difference in your writing, familiarize you with the most recent movements in the field of poetry, and allow you to network among poets, editors, and publishers. The story of Gwendolyn Brooks, one of today's most prominent poets and African-American voices, helps illustrate how powerful a good workshop can be. Even as child, Brooks possessed poetic talent. At thirteen years of age, she had a poem published in *American Childhood,* a respected magazine. In high school she was introduced to James Weldon Johnson and Langston Hughes, the latter of whom played a great role in Brooks' life by writing about her in his newspaper column. In her late teenage years, Brooks published over seventy-five poems in one of Chicago's African-American newspapers, the *Defender.* However, after junior college, Brooks did not get the job that she wanted at the *Defender,* so she employed herself with typing jobs until she got married and raised two children. She stopped publishing. Years later, Brooks and her husband decided to join Inez Cunningham Stark's poetry workshop. While participating, they read and wrote modern poetry. After this training, Brooks' career skyrocketed. Within several years, she had won numerous awards, had her first book published, received the Guggenheim Fellowship, and was granted $1,000 from the American Academy of Arts. That workshop on modern poetry seemed to give her the extra something necessary to trigger a wonderful and long career.

The anxiety to get into print can overshadow your drive to develop your skills adequately. Editors complain that too many poets submit their work for publication before it is ready. Allow yourself time for your craft to mature. After working on your poems, and even coming up with new ones, begin the Square One System again. The next time around, it will be easier. You know the drill.

OTHER OPTIONS TO CONSIDER

If you are not finding success with the small and literary magazines, or if you are finding limited success but want to try other options, consider the ideas described below. Some of them warrant keeping your poetry in hand, while others introduce you to new fields and markets.

Enter Lots of Contests

Actually, poets seeking publication should be entering contests from the very beginning, but contests are especially helpful if you haven't had any luck with the small magazines and journals. From contests advertised in writers' magazines to Haiku contests posted on soymilk containers (yes, this is real!), you will be shocked at the number of opportunities. The large body of competitions opens up a whole new market space for you. Try your hand at different types, from local to national contests.

A great source for finding legitimate contests is *The Complete Guide to Literary Contests*, by William F. Fabio and James M. Plagianos. This helpful text lists hundreds of competitions (though not all for poets), the rules and prizes, limited submission guidelines, entry forms where possible, deadlines, and more. Contact information is provided for further information, including names, addresses, phone and fax numbers, and e-mail and website addresses, when available.

Take Note

Contests are a great way for poets to break into print, and entry fees should be reasonable. But be leery of scams. Do not take part in any contest that requires extravagant fees. Always be sure to confirm that a contest is legitimate.

The Complete Guide to Literary Contests is an easy-to-use, trustworthy guide. Begin at the Table of Contents, where sponsors and awards (referring to fellowships and grants) are listed alphabetically in boldface type. Underneath each sponsor name is an italicized description of the category handled in the contest. For example, you'll find descriptions such as: *Poetry, Fiction, and One-Liners; Unpublished Poetry; Published and Unpublished Poetry and Chapbooks.* This makes it easier to identify which contests are appropriate for you. Next, the name of the contest is given, with a page number on which to find further information. In each detailed entry within the body of the book, you can read about the sponsoring organization. The scope of contests range from national competitions, such as those hosted by the National Federation of State Poetry Societies, Inc., to state university competitions like those at the State University of New York at Farmingdale, to contests sponsored by presses such as Story Line Press.

Other great sources of information on legitimate contests are the market resources listed in Chapter 3. For example, *Poet's Market* has a great section on "Contests & Awards." Let's look at a couple of examples, just to give you an idea of the different types of opportunities that are available. Notice the difference in submission requests, entry fees, and monetary awards.

There are highly specific contests that look for particular writing levels, ages, subjects, etc. The annual Capricorn Poetry Award, sponsored by The Writer's Voice in New York City, is an example of such a competition. It awards $2,000 to an up-and-coming poet who is over forty years of age. Participants are instructed to submit a forty-eight to sixty-eight page manuscript, at least 50-percent of which must be unpublished.

Then there are the open contests. The Milton Dorfman National Poetry Prize, sponsored by the Rome Art & Community Center in St. Rome, New York, gives $500, $200, and $100 awards for unpublished poetry, and requires no experience on the part of the poet.

As a final example, consider the Poetic Potpourri Quarterly Contests, which take place in Lattimore, North Carolina. Prizes are: $75, $50, $25, and three Honorable Mentions. This contest is open to both new and experienced poets. Furthermore, both previously published poems and simultaneous submissions are accepted. You can send any number of poems, any style, any length, any subject. You certainly have a good understanding of the varied contest opportunities by now.

Don't forget the Internet as a source for contest information, as well. Many e-zines and other literary sites hold poetry contests. Even Blue Mountain Arts, a greeting card and e-card company, runs a poetry contest right online. Winners of this particular contest not only get monetary prizes and have their work posted at the site, but also have their poems set as poetry e-cards that viewers can choose to send. Finally, check local newspapers, ads in writers' magazines (for national and international contests), bulletin boards at libraries, and postings at college and university English departments.

Many contests require reading or entry fees. This is how the sponsors pay the prizes and the judges. You can find lots of competitions that don't charge more than $5 to $10. Certainly don't trust any contest that requires astronomical fees. And never blindly enter a contest, for frauds and scams abound. Scam artists know that poets face a tough market. They also know how badly many poets want to break into print. So poetry contests are a breeding ground for con games. If you are interested in a contest, investigate the sponsor by checking reputable resources. Send for as much information as possible, and read the rules with a suspicious eye. Some scam contests even go so far as to advertise in reputable newspapers and magazines; these crooks make enough money to offset ad costs. Play it smart and triple check a contest's legitimacy before you send money.

Contest con artists often repeatedly change the name of the organizations, so that the scams can't be traced back to them. They use very general words in their fake titles, such as "International Poet Awards" and "Famous Writer Competition." After collecting bags of money, these scammers disappear. By the time the poets recognize the hoax, the "sponsors" are long gone.

To give you a better idea of how such frauds work, let's consider a typical scenario. First, the swindler prints a nice-looking ad in several magazines, convincing the poet to send a couple of poems, along with an author biography and an entry fee. If the fee is $10, by the time 400 poets respond, the crook has $4,000 in the bank. Regardless of the quality of the poems—for they remain unread—each poet receives a letter in the mail dripping with sugary praise and mountain-high promises. The poet is told that she has been selected as a winner and is on her way to obtaining a great title, such as Poet of the Year or International Poet. The letter contains an invitation to a winners' weekend and a list of already-won prizes, as well as several grand prizes for which the poet is now eligible. But the letter also asks for a $500 registration fee, not to mention the fact that the poet has to make her own travel arrangements. If the poet bites and sends the additional funds, she is likely not to hear from the sponsor again. There is also a chance that the winners' weekend will take place, but the shoddy accommodations and flimsy gifts certainly won't justify the funds that the poet supplied. You can imagine how much money the con artists are making, even if only one-sixth of the entrants fall for the scheme.

If you've been taken in, don't beat yourself up. Simply learn from the mistake. And if you have not fallen for the "too-good-to-be-true" scams, keep trusting your instincts! You can't be too careful when it comes to contests.

Use the Internet

In Chapter 2, we briefly discussed the latest craze in poetry publishing—the Internet's varied and sundry collection of webzines. The staff members of these webzines or e-zines review and select poetry submissions, although many of the editors

> ### Helpful Hint
>
> If you have fallen for a contest scam, don't beat yourself up. Learn from your experience, and put more time into researching contests in the future. Do not give up on this area of opportunity for breaking into print.

serve without pay. And speaking of pay, you won't be getting a check in the mail if your work does get accepted. However, you will get exposure and feedback. The chosen poems are placed on the websites, and many e-zines archive old issues online. The majority of e-zines ask that you include your e-mail address in the author biography information, so that readers can provide you with feedback and send you questions.

While many webzines get flooded with submissions, new online magazines are always popping up. This market offers a whole new battery of publications for you to try. Granted, you will not have the traditional dream of being "in print," but publishing online is a pretty powerful thing too! Millions of people can read your work at the click of a mouse. So try surfing the web for poetry and literary e-zines. Believe me, you'll find a lot.

It is best to offer a few examples in order to illustrate this rather new type of publishing. _Prairie Poetry_ is a quality and specialized webzine that seeks poetry reflecting the spirit of North America's flatland. This e-zine is open to authors from all regions and is published monthly, except for the month of August. Many writers submit to this site, and, therefore, after acceptance, it could be up to four months until the poem appears online. Notification is sent to the accepted authors over e-mail. Submission guidelines are available at the site.

The _Mystic River Review_ is a beautiful e-zine dedicated to poetry, fiction, and essays. Sponsored by the Arlington Center for the Arts in Arlington, Massachusetts, this webzine offers a simple, elegant approach to modern online literature. It is a welcome break from e-zines that sacrifice sophistication for flashy graphics. According to the site, the staff generally looks for poetry that is "clear, non-sentimental, and emotionally alive." The _Mystic River Review_ is web-published two to three times annually. Poets can submit up to four poems of 100 or less lines each.

Also take a look at the following e-zines for more examples of online publications: _Big Bridge_, _Poetfest_, and _The Rose & Thorn Literary Ezine_. These will give you a good idea of the varied

> ## Helpful Hint
>
> While concentrating on strategy for publication, it is easy to forget the beauty of the poetry craft itself. Always remember that the sheer writing of a poem with which you are happy—publications and professionals aside— inherently proves success and provides satisfaction.

approaches available. You can find the web addresses in the Resource Directory beginning on page 147.

There's also the option of learning how to develop your own web page, or even your own webzine. You may know a group of writers who would like to attempt putting an e-zine together. You can find some "how to" instructions at *Factsheet 5's* website (http://www.factsheet5.com).

Self-Publish Your Work

The nice part about self-publishing is that you can publish your book within a couple of months, and you pick and choose which companies to use for which services.

There have been situations in which a poet gets refused by countless magazines and publishers, but then successfully self-publishes and promotes her own book. This certainly doesn't happen for every self-publisher. But if you have some extra money to play with, and if you have a knack for publicity, then you have a shot. The important part is to fully research this option before investing *any* money.

The industry of self-publishing is discussed in Chapter 2 (pages 34 to 36). There are lots of details involved in publishing your own book, be it a chapbook or a full manuscript. First and foremost, comparison shop! Collect data on pricing and print runs from as many printers as possible. Price typesetters as well, if you require one. Look at sample work from every company that you are considering.

There are many ways that presses can fool you into paying more than you expect. For example, a company might advertise that they will print 200 copies of a fifty-page book for $2.00 per copy. You might think, "Not bad! I can set aside $400." But the details reveal that this price is for camera-ready copy only; you'll have to have the manuscript fully typeset and formatted before this base price begins. Then there's the binding fee, the cover fee, and the shipping and packaging fees, to name a few. You have multiple options, too. If you want sturdier paper, add more money. If you want colored ink on the cover, add more money. You'll be bombarded with 101 extra service choices. Protect yourself by reading about the business and understanding the industry vocabulary before even considering a deal.

Furthermore, avoid getting roped into purchasing more than you need or desire. For example, don't get swindled into purchasing costly posters and bookmarks as "part of the package." You will not be able to put them or send them anywhere until you have made a name for yourself. Keep in mind the fact that you'll probably be handing these copies out as free gifts and selling them after poetry readings. You do not want to get carried away with glamour at this point.

The nice part about self-publishing is that you can publish your book within a couple of months, and you pick and choose what companies to use for what services. You are not bound by pre-set packages, as you would be if working with subsidy and vanity presses. And unlike working with traditional publishing houses, you get 100 percent of the profits. In addition, self-publishing is respected. Authors who do it well can produce a quality product for a reasonable price.

Self-publishing is not easy business. The bills add up and the responsibility is great. Published books also need ISBN numbers and Library of Congress Catalog Card Numbers. (These are details you cannot forget. Many publishing facilities can help you with these processes for additional fees.) As soon as the book is printed, you have to start promoting your collection with energy and aggression. The reality is, you are solely in charge of marketing, distribution, storage, and additional print runs. So make sure that you have all the time and money it takes before entering into the process, and don't get carried away with sweeping expectations. There is always the chance that your book will become popular and a publisher will pursue you in the future. Just realize that this does not happen to *most* poets.

There are some striking success stories. Walt Whitman, for example, self-published his first collection. Editor Joel Conarroe, in *Six American Poets: An Anthology,* writes, "The year 1855 stands as a red-letter date in American literature, for it was

It will be a great challenge to effectively publicize a self-published poetry book. Self-published poetry books are the least likely of all self-published texts to generate a substantial income.

Walt Whitman was born in Brooklyn in 1819. Whitman started several careers—including that of printer, teacher, and clerk for the Department of the Interior—and eventually turned to journalism as a full-time profession. He is best known for his poetry collection *Leaves of Grass,* of which he published several editions. Whitman struggled to support himself throughout most of his life, sometimes surviving on "purses" sent by other writers. In the early 1870s, Whitman settled in Camden, New Jersey, near his brother. He died in 1892.

when the thirty-six-year-old poet published at his own expense a ninety-five-page 'language experiment,' made up of twelve untitled poems (and a long preface), called *Leaves of Grass.*" The rest is history. However, the collection met with plenty of adversity at first. While Ralph Waldo Emerson apparently praised the work, James Russell Lowell and John Greenleaf Whittier were among the writers who despised it. Whitman also lost a government clerkship job due to his risqué verses. At one point, the book was banned in Boston. So this is not only an example of successful self-publishing, but of how history can prove reviewers to be off the mark.

Renowned poet Nikki Giovanni is another self-publishing success, and a much more recent one at that. Ms. Giovanni's story begins in the 1960s, when she began pursuing writing as a career. While attending the School of Fine Arts at Columbia University, Giovanni was told she could not write. But she borrowed money to self-publish her first collection, *Black Feeling, Black Talk.* Several years later, while teaching at Queens College, Giovanni convinced a club manager to allow her to throw a book party. She did a good job of publicizing the event. A reporter from *The New York Times* became curious and attended Giovanni's reading, which drew a huge crowd. His story about the event, with photos, ended up on the front cover of the Metro section of the newspaper. Over the next eight months, Giovanni sold 10,000 copies of her self-published book. A grant from the Harlem Council of the Arts followed. The poet used the money to publish her second volume, called *Black Judgement.* Her career continues to soar.

The Resource Directory, which begins on page 147, recommends several books on self-publishing. There are quite a few guides available at bookstores and libraries. Plus, the Internet offers a lot of information on self-publishing. Some company names, just to start you on gathering information, are Morris Publishing and Brown Books. See the Resource Directory for contact information.

Yolande Cornelia "Nikki" Giovanni was born in Knoxville, Tennessee in 1943, and raised in Ohio. After being told she couldn't write by a professor at Columbia University, Giovanni went on to publish several poetry collections and receive the NAACP Image Award for Literature, and the Langston Hughes award for Distinguished Contributions to Arts and Letters. Her poetry has been deeply influenced by her African-American heritage.

Submit Verse to Greeting Card Companies

Are you a wordsmith? Can you say a lot in a little space? If so, consider sending freelance submissions to greeting card companies. The process is similar to that of submitting poetry to magazines. You should definitely research the individual companies, write away for submission guidelines or visit the companies' websites, and follow all instructions carefully. In addition, just as when submitting poetry, spend the majority of your efforts on small- and medium-sized outfits that happily accept unsolicited work from freelancers.

There are numerous greeting card companies established throughout the United States and Canada. In fact, according to Valerie Zehl's *Writer's Digest* article titled "Crafting Greeting Cards That Sell," there are over 1,500 small- and medium-sized greeting card companies! Zehl explains that many of these will offer about $25 for each verse or idea they accept. Larger companies pay writers from $100 to $150 per verse, on average. The entire industry generates over $7 billion per year, so it can afford to compensate those who supply the wit, puns, and sweet-nothings.

Valerie Zehl, mentioned above, reveals that 80 to 85 percent of the greeting card industry is controlled by three major companies: Hallmark; American Greetings; and Gibson Greetings. These large companies don't rely on slush-pile submissions. For example, Hallmark employs an in-house staff to carry out the creative process, and does not accept freelance submissions. American Greetings and Gibson Greetings do read unsolicited submissions, but the opportunities are very limited.

There's no doubt that your odds of selling verse are greater when pitching to smaller companies. Also, submit to e-card companies. This is a great, and growing, business. In "E-Cards: A New Frontier for Freelancers," article author Jaime Seba takes a look at eGreetings Network. This company—one of the largest in the industry—sends out approximately 100,000 e-cards per

Helpful Hint

When submitting verse to greeting card companies, follow a process similar to that of poetry submission. Send your work to the small- and medium-sized companies; always obtain submission guidelines; and select a niche that is most compatible with your particular writing style.

Many of today's independent card companies look for relaxed, conversational verse, not only for significant occasions such as birthdays and anniversaries, but for everyday occurrences and personal issues. For example, the following is text from an "apology" card, simply communicating that the sender overreacted and wants to send loving thoughts:

*Sometimes my heart
runs ahead of me,
and my mind races
forward to catch up.
But I'm learning it's better
to simply slow down
and wait for my heart
to find me again.*

*I'm sorry I reacted
so quickly.
I can't wait to slow down
in your arms.*

day. Payment policy involves royalties; the author of a given card gets paid according to how many times the card is ordered.

Some companies look for "warm and fuzzy" verse, while others accept adult humor only, and still others want non-rhyming, modern verse. Preferences and policies vary so much that submission guidelines and research is absolutely necessary. *Poet's Market 2000* contains an essay by Sandra Miller-Louden, titled *"Poetry does not equal success when writing for greeting cards."* According to Miller-Louden, most of the standard, rhymed poetry you find on greeting cards is developed by staff writers at one of the "Big Three" headquarters—Hallmark, American Greetings, or Gibson Greetings. So that particular niche is not too promising. However, humorous phrases and contemporary prose are desirable. Miller-Louden writes, "Mid-size companies want and need your freelance work. What they don't want or need is your rhymed, metered poetry." Conversational, clever, and easy verse is much more marketable.

There are some great resources available to help you with greeting card writing and the process of submitting it. The Resource Directory beginning on page 147 includes several books and websites that will help you.

Experiment With Another Genre

You certainly have an interest in writing. Why not try other types—children's literature, freelance articles, short stories, even novel-length works? You may have categorized yourself as a poet because you've been writing rhyme since you were young, or because your favorite writers are poets. Whatever the reason, don't be so quick to pigeonhole yourself. It can't hurt to try other modes.

Sometimes poets hold too tightly to their label as poets. There is something romantic, timeless, and profound about being a poet. But *every* type of writing opens your mind. A voice is a voice, no matter what the language, page format, or style.

While considering different types of writing, have you thought about songwriting? Whether or not you write music, you can try a few lyrics. Songwriting is about as lucrative as poetry. Very few people make money from it. But if you love the rhythm and meter of well-developed verse, and if you have an ear for the musical, why not find out more about this field? Some helpful books on this subject are found in the Resource Directory under "Guidebooks on Other Options for Poets," beginning on page 165.

Take Part in Craft-Making

If you want to stick with writing verse, you do have the option of putting your efforts toward craft projects. Consider scouting around for local artists who work on projects such as calendars, gift books, and gift baskets. Attend local craft fairs and speak with some of the artists. Maybe a photographer needs someone to write short passages to accompany her calendar photos. Perhaps a doll-maker could use a creative writer to compose children's poems to tuck into the dolls' arms. Even tee-shirt captions are an option! Don't be afraid to propose such ideas.

If you have the funds, you can also self-publish a chapbook (defined on page 30). Purchase a *very* short print run—maybe fifty copies. Rent a table at a local craft fair, or even a shelf at a shop that allows artists to rent space. It is preferable to get a few artists to share the table or shelf with you. Therefore, you will be offering a variety of products, increasing the likelihood that a passerby will stop and look. Once you have a potential customer in your space, you can promote the little books. The customer may be looking for stocking stuffers at Christmas, or for a little gift book to attach to a friend's package for Valentine's Day.

If nothing else, work your poetry into other crafts that you enjoy. Do you needlepoint? Stitch out one of your poems for your child or your friend. Do you do calligraphy? Include hand-written copies of an original poem in your holiday cards to spe-

Helpful Hint

Don't box yourself in! If your poetry efforts prove fruitless, experiment with other writing options, from short stories, to tee-shirt slogans, to photography captions.

cial people. They will love the extra touch because they love you. Your words will mean a lot to them, whether they are in perfect meter or not.

Offer Your Time as a Volunteer

After writing poetry for quite some time, you've surely come to realize that writing is a healing art, as well as a way to develop your communication skills. There are many people who can benefit from your love of writing and your skills with language. If you like working with words and sharing your passion with others, consider volunteering with local writing programs for the underprivileged or the literacy-challenged.

Often, facilities and programs such as prisons, foster-home services, schools, and community centers offer writing courses or workshops for those who want to learn more about expressing themselves. Talk to the personnel and see if they'd like some help. Explain that you have been writing poetry for a long time and would like to share your passion for creative writing with others. You will have great fun bringing out the poet in others, while celebrating the poet in you.

CONCLUSION

Hopefully, this chapter has given you some helpful perspectives and a few good ideas, whether you ultimately decide to further pursue the publication of your poetry or to branch into something different. If your poetry does start to scale the ladder of publication, be proud and take the power of your gift seriously. Continue to work hard to plant the seeds of your poetry, and allow yourself to fully enjoy the fruits of your labor when they ripen. No words can truly explain the exhilaration of a realized dream—not even poetry.

CONCLUSION

This book was designed solely to improve your chances of getting your poetry published. It lets you in on the basics of the poetry publishing business, virtually sets up a bookshelf of market materials for you to reference, and provides you with a step-by-step system for getting your work onto the editors' desks in professional form. While concentrating on *strategy* for publication, it is easy to forget the beauty of the poetry *craft* itself. Always remember that the sheer writing of a poem with which *you* are happy publications and professionals aside— inherently proves success and provides satisfaction.

That being said, seeing your work recognized and offered to others in print is a wonderful thing—no doubt about it. And if your work has what it takes, then following the organized and proactive Square One System will get you there. There's nothing like the first time that a poet sees his or her poetry lines in professional print. No matter who the poet is, the reaction is one of honor, excitement, pride, and hope, as demonstrated below in an excerpt from a letter written by Robert Frost. (The letter is printed in its entirety in *Robert Frost: Poetry and Prose*, edited by

Edward Connery Lathem and Lawrance Thompson.) Frost sent it to the editor of *The Independent* (a national publication) in 1894, after learning that the publication had accepted his poem, "My Butterfly," for print. This was Frost's first acceptance and, as you will read, the poet was overwhelmed:

> The memory of your note will be a fresh pleasure
> to me when I awaken for a good many mornings
> to come. . . . The poem you have is the first of
> mine that any publication has accepted. . . .
> As for submitting more of my work, you may
> imagine I shall be only too glad to avail myself
> of your kindly interest. . . .

Incidentally, Frost received a $15.00 check for his poem. Not bad! Frost's words of humble exhilaration remind us that, along the walls of our efforts, there are doors. Seek publication with courage, approach it with persistence, and truly enjoy the moment when one of the keys in your pocket fits.

RESOURCE DIRECTORY

Following are some groups and contacts that are helpful for poets who would like to get published. Please note that any contact information is subject to change. Be sure to contact each organization to verify the information you need.

POETS/WRITERS ORGANIZATIONS

Academy of American Poets
584 Broadway, Suite 1208
New York, NY 10012
Phone: 212–274–0343
Fax: 212–274–9427
Website: http://www.poets.org

This organization, founded in 1934, offers support to poets at all career stages and encourages the appreciation of poetry among the public. It is the largest organization dedicated to poets and their work. The Academy of American Poets sponsors award contests, readings, lectures, symposiums, and more. The Academy of American Poets' website contains information on the awards, programs, and membership benefits. Also on the website, you can find: a calendar of events; news on National Poetry Month; "Find a Poet," through which biographies and links for individual poets are provided; poetry exhibits; an online bookstore; and discussion forums through which writers can post their work for review by fellow members.

National Federation of State Poetry Societies, Inc.
2712 Scott Avenue
Fort Worth, TX 76103
Phone: 817–535–7304; 605–768–2127
Fax: 817–531–6593
Website: http://www.wpacf.org/natl.htm
E-mail: JFS@flash.net

The NFSPS, founded in 1959, focuses on enhancing the significance of poetry as it affects our national culture. This organization seeks to form a community for poetry groups across the nation. Most states are affiliated with the NFSPS, and poetry groups in states that are not involved with the NFSPS can contact the organization for guidance. Also, individuals interested in forming a poetry group in a state that has not registered with the NFSPS can contact the organization for help. You can trust that groups registered with NFSPS are quality, respectable societies. Most legitimate state poetry societies belong to this organization, but not all. The quarterly bulletin *Strophes* advertises contests run by member societies. NFSPS's annual meeting is held in a different city each year. The organization also sponsors fifty national contests annually. Call the NFSPS for information on your state poetry society.

National Writers Association
1450 S. Havana, Suite 424
Aurora, CO 80012
Phone: 303–751–7844
Fax: 303–751–8593
Website: http://www.nationalwriters.com

The National Writers Association, founded in 1937, counts both new and famous writers—including poets and playwrights—among its members. Membership entitles you to receive a bi-monthly newsletter, *Authorship,* and admittance to the National Writers Association's annual conference, usually held in June. It also offers support and guidance services, such as peer reviews of your work, contract reading, networking among members, and listings of available jobs in the fields of writing and publishing. The website contains an online bookstore, e-mail addresses of helpful staff members, and information on the NWA Press.

Poetry Society of America
15 Gramercy Park
New York, NY 10003
Phone: 212–254–9628
Phone: 800–USA–POEM (for free brochure)
Fax: 212–673–2352
Website: http://www.poetrysociety.org
E-mail: poetrysocy@aol.com

This organization, founded in 1910, endeavors to extend the awareness and appreciation of poetry nationwide. Just a few of the early members of this group were Robert Frost, Langston Hughes, Marianne Moore, Ezra Pound, and Wallace Stevens. Among its services, the Poetry Society of America conducts a national series of poetry readings, mounts posters of poetry in public transportation systems, runs an educational poetry series on cable television, sponsors annual poetry contests, holds seminars and festivals, and publishes a newsletter. The website contains information on membership benefits, such as a subscription to the journal, *Crossroads;* a calendar of events; discounts to readings; and exemption from contest fees. It also gives information on: awards; journals and literary magazines; poet colonies; poetry organizations; conferences; festivals; poetry publishers and small presses; MFA programs in poetry; and other helpful Internet sites.

Poets & Writers, Inc.

72 Spring Street
New York, NY 10012
Phone: 212–226–3586
Fax: 212–226–3963
Website: http://www.pw.org

Poets & Writers, Inc., founded in 1970, encourages the endeavors of poets and fiction writers, offering them guidance, market tips, and much more. This organization publishes *Poets & Writers Magazine* (discussed under "Writers' Magazines") and other publications, and provides support for readings and workshops. There is no membership involved. Simply contact the organization for information, events, etc. The website is a wonderful resource, providing: magazine excerpts; publishing advice; a "Speakeasy" forum; contest listings; a directory of writers; an online bookstore; information on grants and awards; classifieds; helpful links to other Internet sites; and more.

MARKET RESOURCE BOOKS

Directory of Literary Magazines: Complete Information on More Than 600 U.S. and Foreign Magazines That Publish Poetry, Fiction, and Essay

by the Council of Literary Magazines and Presses. Wakefield, RI: Asphodel Press, updated periodically.

The first benefit of this resource guide is that it deals exclusively with magazines, making it very appropriate for the poet who is just starting to break into print. Each magazine entry includes: the editor's name; the publication address, phone number, fax, e-mail and website (where possible); a list of literary genres published in the magazine; a description of the publication; the subscription price; the names of several recent contributors; annual figures on submissions received and accepted; the publication's policy on simultaneous submissions; reporting time; the first year of publication; frequency of publication; and circulation data. Although it provides a Geographical Index, this directory has no subject index to the poetry magazines, so you'll have to flip through it. In addition, no submission guidelines are listed. *The Directory of Literary Magazines* does offer foreign market listings though, and an easy-to-read "list" format, rather than small-print paragraphs.

The International Directory of Little Magazines and Small Presses

by Len Fulton, ed. Paradise, CA: Dustbooks, updated annually.

This resource book offers several hundred pages of listings, as well as a Regional Index and a Subject Index. For each entry, you'll find: name of the press; name of the editor(s), contact information, including the address, phone number, and any other available modes of contact; the year the publication or press was founded; a description of the type of poetry desired;

comments, including the names of several recently published contributors; circulation information; the number of issues published per year; publication size, page count, and printing method; and response time. The international listings introduce you to some markets that you may not otherwise find. The Subject Index will guide you to entries that are helpful for poets. (Look under "Poetry" to start.) Be aware that submission guidelines are not given, nor is the information on whether or not an individual market is open to beginners.

Literary Market Place: The Directory of the International Book Publishing Industry

New Providence, NJ: R.R. Bowker, updated annually.

The *LMP* is useful to the poet who is ready to embark on the publication of a collection, after having gained considerable publication credits through literary magazine markets. The *LMP* is widely used within the publishing industry, and is updated annually. It provides extensive lists of book publishers, from the largest commercial publishing houses to small presses. For every publisher listed, various modes of contact are offered, as well as editor names. Publishers are listed alphabetically. To find publishers of poetry, look under "poetry" in the Subject Index. You can also find information on e-publishers in this book, as well as what publishing houses have received awards. Also contained in the *LMP* are names of editorial services, printing facilities, and the like. The information is current and reliable.

Poet's Market

by Chantelle Bentley, ed. Cincinnati, OH: Writer's Digest Books, updated periodically.

The most thorough resource book available, *Poet's Market* contains everything from publication tips, to helpful essays, to hundreds of pages dedicated to literary magazine and press markets. Each market entry lets you know: whether the publication or press is open to beginners; how specialized the publication or press is; and if the publication or press has special features like international circulation, online publication, and awards. Every entry includes an address, phone number, website (where possible), editor's name, and a description of the type and style of poetry published within its pages. Submission guidelines are provided, as well. In addition, you will often find details on the size and circulation of publications. Be sure to look at the sections concerning contests and awards, conferences and workshops, writers' organizations, and arts councils. Suggested publications and websites lead you to further sources. The lists of markets that take e-mail submissions, publishers who publish chapbooks, and publishers who publish poetry books, as well as a number of other helpful indexes, are invaluable to the poet who is on a time budget.

Ulrich's International Periodicals Directory
by the Bowker International Serials Database. New Providence, NJ: R.R. Bowker, updated periodically.

A hardcover research text, *Ulrich's International Periodicals Directory* lists international serials and is a good resource for poets who want to delve into lesser known and foreign markets. Look under "Poetry" in the "Classified List of Serials" and you'll find a list of poetry publications. Once you have the names, you can find each entry, according to title, in the alphabetically organized volumes. The entries vary in the amount and type of information they hold, but usually the following is provided: frequency of publication; publisher's address and country code; and further contact information, possibly including telephone number, fax, e-mail, and website address. Other commonly listed information includes: the first year of publication; the number of issues published per year; and circulation details. Literary editors' names are not listed, but special features—for example, the printing of illustrations—are likely to be mentioned. Plus, many listings give a general description of the type of poetry published in the serial, and often tell whether or not the publication is open to beginners. *Ulrich's* does list some e-magazines. No submission guidelines are provided. The data covers only the bare basics.

The Writer's Handbook

by Sylvia K. Burack, ed. Boston, MA: The Writer, Inc., 1999.

A variety of literary markets are addressed in *The Writer's Handbook,* among which are poetry markets. Before you get into the individual market entries, flip through the numerous short chapters that cover topics on the actual writing. In fact, there is a section just for poets. The second part of the book contains thousands of markets, but only some of these are applicable to poetry writers. Turn to the section on poetry and you will find that most of the recommended markets are for college, small, and literary magazines. Each entry includes: publisher's name and address; editor's name; description of the type of poetry published; and payment issues, if applicable. This book gives you just the basics to get your research started. You'll have to pursue submission guidelines on your own, as well as whether or not each listed publication is open to beginners. Absolutely no vanity or subsidy presses are included in this resource, nor magazines that charge fees for reading submissions. There are helpful sections on literary competitions, greeting card markets, writers' colonies, writers' conferences, state arts councils, writers' organizations, and literary book publishers, as well.

WRITERS' MAGAZINES

Poets & Writers Magazine
PO Box 543
Mount Morris, IL 61054
Phone: 815–734–1123
Website: http://www.pw.org

A bimonthly magazine produced by Poets & Writers, Inc. *Poets & Writers* is probably the most helpful periodical on the market for poets. This magazine is available at all major bookstores and libraries. The above-listed address is for subscription requests and questions.

The Writer
120 Boylston Street
Boston, MA 02116–4615
Phone: 617–423–3157
Website: http://www.channel1.com/thewriter/
E-mail: writer@user1.channel1.com

A monthly magazine produced by The Writer, Inc. This magazine is available at major bookstores and some libraries.

Writer's Digest
Box 2123
Harlan, IA 51593
Phone: 800–333–0133
Website: http://www.writersdigest.com

A monthly magazine produced by F&W Publications, Inc. This magazine is available at all major bookstores and libraries.

Writers' Journal
PO Box 394
Perham, MN 56573–0394
Phone: 218–346–7921
Website: http://www.sowashco.com/writersjournal/
E-mail: writersjournal@wadena.net

A bimonthly magazine produced by Val-Tech Media. This magazine is available at major bookstores and some libraries.

CONTEST INFORMATION RESOURCE

See the sections on poetry organizations and market resource books for additional sources of contest information.

The Complete Guide to Literary Contests
Compiled by Literary Fountain, William F. Fabio, Hames M. Plagianos. Amherst, NY: Prometheus Books, 1999.

This guide lists deadlines, addresses, and sponsor information for literary contests. Look for the category of "poetry." Where possible, names, addresses, phone and fax numbers, and e-mail and website addresses are given.

ADDITIONAL HELPFUL WEBSITES

Amateur Poetry: Poetry Market List
http://www.amateurpoetry.com

The "market list" at this site names several markets for unpublished poets, including descriptions and links that will provide further information. It's a good idea to check this site periodically for leads on new publications. The site also provides information on a free contest, writing tips, publishing tips, and more.

Electronic Poetry Center, SUNY Buffalo

http://wings.buffalo.edu/epc/

The State University of New York, Buffalo, provides a wonder-ful resource site for poets. This website contains long lists of both e-zines and print magazines, and allows you to click on the publication name for a link to more information. Some links go right to the publications' home pages, which offer extensive instructions on submission guidelines and on the publications themselves. Where a home page is not available, as is the case for a number of print magazines, an information page is offered.

LitLine: A Not-For-Profit Website for the Independent Literary Community

http://www.litline.org/

LitLine's site provides Internet links to hundreds of small press-es and print journals, literary organizations, and other helpful resources. News on conferences and events is also available. This is a great website to visit for up-to-date information.

ShawGuides: The Guide to Writers Conferences

http://www.Shawguides.com/writing/

ShawGuides is an easy-to-use resource that helps you find con-ferences, workshops, seminars, and writers' retreats that are appropriate for your particular needs. You can type in your state and/or region, and then click on the month and the activities in which you are interested.

Web Del Sol

http://webdelsol.com

Web Del Sol contains a wealth of information, offering sum-maries of specific print magazines and small presses, e-zines, and university creative writing programs. It hosts twenty mag-azines, and publishes poetry on the Editor's Picks page, as well.

There are online chapbooks to read, fiction and poetry reviews, news, and links to other great sites and online workshops. For example, you can click into "Writer's Block," which is a space for posting your poems and getting feedback from other writers. Web Del Sol also offers a monthly newsletter, titled *Electronic Literary Arts Newsletter (ELAN),* and chat rooms.

GUIDEBOOKS AND INFORMATION SOURCES FOR WRITING POETRY

The Art and Craft of Poetry: What Works, What Doesn't and Why, With Methods to Generate Poems and Examples from Shakespeare to Olds

by Michael J. Bugeja. Cincinnati, OH: Writer's Digest Books, 1994.

Bugeja's comprehensive and practical book includes great advice on: how to generate marketable ideas; the basics of poetry as a craft; and exercises to improve your writing. There are lots of example poems, as well as comments and advice from today's top poets. It's an informative and an interesting read.

How to Write Poetry: Learn What Makes a Good Poem— and How to Express Yourself Through Poetry, Third Edition

by Nancy Bogen. New York, NY: Macmillan, 1998.

This book discusses everything from the study of words, to style choices, to literary techniques. The discussions on rhythm, meter, rhyme, and many forms of poetry are valuable for the writer who is trying to improve and formalize his or her work.

The Poet's Companion: A Guide to the Pleasures of Writing Poetry

by Kim Addonizio and Dorianne Laux. New York, NY: WW Norton & Company, 1997.

The Poet's Companion begins with the process of selecting subjects for poetry. It then moves to a discussion of the craft itself, and offers chapters on effective writing techniques. Realistic viewpoints on writer's block, self-doubt, the e-publishing world, and more is provided. You will also find helpful writing exercises and lots of information on the publishing process.

The Practice of Poetry: Writing Exercises from Poets Who Teach

by Robin Behn and Chase Twichell, eds. New York, NY: HarperPerennial, 1992.

The contributors to this book are poetry teachers who have spent much time developing the best ways to guide poets to improvement. *The Practice of Poetry* is chock-full of helpful essays and exercises. Collect tips on triggering imagination, revising your work, and everything in-between.

GUIDEBOOKS AND INFORMATION SOURCES FOR SELF-PUBLISHING

The Complete Guide to Self-Publishing: Everything You Need to Know to Write, Publish, Promote, and Sell Your Own Book, Third Edition

by Tom Ross and Marilyn Ross. Cincinnati, OH: Writer's Digest, 1994.

The authors of this comprehensive text are cofounders of About Books, Inc.—a writing, publishing, and marketing consulting service located in Buena Vista, Colorado. Their book gives in-depth advice on the self-publishing of a number of writing genres, including poetry. The realistic approach is enlightening. Among many topics, the following are discussed: how to take low risks while gaining profits; e-marketing; economical tips on design and printing; starting your own publishing company; publicity strategies; etc. Only a certain portion of the material may seem immediately applicable, but it can't hurt to have a wealth of information at your fingertips.

The Self-Publishing Manual: How to Write, Print, & Sell Your Own Book
by Dan Poynter. Santa Barbara, CA: Para Publishing, 1998.

Repeatedly recognized as one of the best step-by-step books on self-publishing over the course of its several editions, *The Self-Publishing Manual* will introduce you to all the issues that you need to consider on this topic. Poynter's book offers great advice on the entire process, from producing a quality manuscript, to printing, selling, and distributing your work. The most recent edition even contains plenty of information on how the Internet and the World Wide Web have affected the publishing industry, and tells you how to work with this vast system to your advantage.

Brown Books
16200 N. Dallas Parkway, Suite 225
Dallas, TX 75248
Phone: 972–381–0009
Fax: 972–248–4336
Website: http://www.brownbooks.com

Brown Books provides clear information for the author who is considering self-publishing. It also offers its customers a variety of options, including help with writing; editing; typesetting; marketing; and distribution.

Morris Publishing
3212 E. Highway 30
Kearney, NE 68847
Phone: 800–650–7888
Fax: 308–237–0263
Website: http://morrispublishing.com
E-mail: publish@morrispublishing.com

This company is an example of a full-service self-publishing company. It offers helpful information on the industry and details the variety of options that are available.

GUIDEBOOKS AND INFORMATION SOURCES FOR E-PUBLISHING

1st Books Library
http://www.1stbooks.com

1st Books is actually a retail site, but it will give you an idea of what kinds of books are currently available for downloading and sale. In addition, you'll get a greater feel for the industry of e-publishing.

Electronic Publishing: The Definitive Guide
by Karen S. Wiesner. Petals of Life Publishing, 1999.

All of the common questions about e-publishing are addressed in this book. Attention is paid to both positives and negatives of the e-publishing industry in language that every reader can understand. Learn how e-publishing works, technically, and what expectations are reasonable. *Electronic Publishing: The Definitive Guide* provides a lengthy list of e-publishers, as well as information on selling and promoting your e-book.

U-Publish.Com: How Individual Writers Can Now Effectively Compete With the Giants of the Publishing Industry by Dan Poynter and Danny O. Snow. 1st Books Library, 2000.

This book is geared toward authors and publishers who want to take advantage of the latest in publishing technologies, especially electronic and print-on-demand techniques. U-Publish.com teaches you how to do the most with a manuscript for the least amount of money. It offers production instruction and marketing methods. The authors are prominent in their fields: Poynter is noted as a top authority on self-publishing, and Snow possesses expertise in the most current publishing trends. See the website associated with this book, http://www.u-publish.com, for more information, free offers, and cutting-edge updates.

InTech Publishing
1749 Overland Street
Fort Worth, TX 76131
Phone: 817–232–3806
Website: http://www.intechpublishing.net

InTech Publishing is a company that digitally publishes accepted book manuscripts. (It also offers Web development and design.) Both published and unpublished works are considered. The manuscript itself is developed into a software program, which is then made available to customers through Internet downloading and, in some cases, CD-ROM. If a book is selected for publication by InTech, all digital costs are covered. InTech pays authors in royalties. For more information, see their helpful website.

E-ZINE SEARCH SITES AND RECOMMENDED PUBLICATIONS

Big Bridge
http://www.bigbridge.org/

Big Bridge is published by an able staff that also founded Big Bridge Press and a couple of small print magazines. This e-zine is an organized, cutting edge webzine that has everything from information on the editors to an online store. Several poets are featured in every edition. *Big Bridge* publishes fiction, nonfiction, essays, journalism, photography, and graphics, as well. Submissions, including simultaneous submissions, are accepted year round.

Electronic Poetry Center
http://wings.buffalo.edu/epc/

The State University of New York, Buffalo, provides a wonderful resource site for poets interested in e-zines and print magazines. See the summary on page 55.

Mystic River Review
http://www.acarts.org/mystic

Sophisticated and well-respected, the *Mystic River Review* accepts submissions of poetry, fiction, and essays. Sponsored by the Arlington Center for the Arts in Arlington, Massachusetts, the *Mystic River Review's* editors generally look for poetry that is "clear, non-sentimental, and emotionally alive." This e-zine is web-published two to three times annually. Poets can submit up to four poems of 100 or less lines each.

Poetfest

http://www.geocities.com/Athens/Acropolis/7101

This is a virtual celebration of poetry maintained, amazingly, by one man. *Poetfest* is published online seasonally, and all levels of poets are encouraged to participate in this continual "series" of poetry. This is one of the most recognized and respected poetry e-zines.

Prairie Poetry

http://www.prairiepoetry.org

Prairie Poetry is a quality and specialized webzine. It publishes poetry that expresses the spirit of North America's open, flat prairie lands. Authors from all regions are encouraged to submit, but poems must fall within this theme.

nice, but not for me, yet. It's complicated, I think.

The Rose & Thorn: A Literary Ezine

http://members.aol.com/Raven763/index.html

This quarterly webzine promotes a mingling of contemporary and traditional prose. The selected poetry is capable of promoting rich thought and imagery. Both new writers and published writers are invited to submit.

RESOURCES FOR LEGAL ISSUES

Every Writer's Guide to Copyright and Publishing Law
by Ellen M. Kozak. Owlet Publishing, 1997.

This approachable text does not overwhelm you with legal terminology; it simplifies the confusing terms and issues that arise for upcoming authors. Some applicable subjects for new writers are U.S. copyright law, including e-copyrights, fair use, and contract information.

***The Writer's Legal Companion: The Complete Handbook
for the Working Writer,*** Third Edition
by Brad Bunnin and Peter Beren. Reading, MA: Perseus Books, 1998.

In the pages of this thorough handbook, you'll find legal advice
on contracts, magazine publishing, copyright law, taxes, and much
more. The glossary of publishing terms is extremely helpful.

U.S. Copyright Office
Library of Congress
101 Independence Avenue, SE
Washington, DC 20559–6000
Phone: 202–707–9100 (to leave a message concerning requests
    for publications and application forms)
Phone: 202–707–3000 (to speak to a staff member for information)
Website: http://lcweb.loc.gov/copyright/

Find a wealth of information on copyright issues and laws at
this site, as well as downloadable versions of forms.

U.S. Post Office
Website: http://www.usps.gov/business/calcs.htm

Access this website for general information on postage fees, or
speak with your local postal service agent.

GUIDEBOOKS ON OTHER OPTIONS FOR POETS

***6 Steps to Songwriting Success: Comprehensive Guide
to Writing and Marketing Hit Songs***
by Jason Blume. New York, NY: Watson-Guptill Publishers, 1999.

This is an easy-to-read, practical approach to writing the type of
song that has "hit" potential. The author has written songs for

some of today's most popular singing artists, and advises from firsthand experience. He offers exercises, self-evaluation check-lists, stories, anecdotes, and more.

The Children's Writer's Reference

by Berthe Amoss and Eric Suben. Cincinnati, OH: Writer's Digest Books Inc., 1999.

This is a helpful and easy-to-read guidebook that touches on many different topics. Some of the subjects discussed are: ideas for subject matter; character, setting, and plot development; insights into children's skills and interests; and formats and word selections.

The Craft and Business of Songwriting

by John Braheny. Cincinnati, OH: Writer's Digest Books Inc., 1995.

Braheny's book organizes the craft of songwriting into helpful principles to offer general guidance, instead of strict rules to box your creative talent. Through his practical writing style, you get a real sense of the options available to you. Equal attention is given to craft and business issues.

How to Write and Sell Greeting Cards, Bumper Stickers, T-Shirts and Other Fun Stuff

by Molly Wigand. Cincinnati, OH: Writer's Digest Books Inc., 1992.

Wigand is a former employee of Hallmark and a freelance writer. She offers exciting advice on available creative avenues for writers: cards; plaques; buttons; bumper stickers; t-shirts; mugs; etc. Learn how to trace trends, how to market your writing, and how to come up with effective ideas. This fun and encouraging book also contains writing exercises.

The Way to Write for Children: An Introduction to the Craft of Writing Children's Literature
by Joan Aiken. New York, NY: St. Martin's Press, 1999.

Aiken first debunks the myth that children's literature is easy to write. She warns authors about the most common misperceptions and mistakes in writing children's literature. Then, Aiken discusses the craft of writing literature for all ages of children, toddlers to teens. Find advice on how to choose a subject, how to create characters, and how to structure plot. Furthermore, learn why certain authors, such as Beatrix Potter and Maurice Sendak, have become so popular.

You Can Write Greeting Cards
by Karen Ann Moore. Cincinnati, OH: Writer's Digest Books Inc., 1999.

The author of this book is very experienced within her field. She offers great instructions and exercises. This guide helps you find your niche and learn how to market within it. Learn about both the creation of greeting card text and the business of selling it.

EFERENCES

BOOKS AND PERIODICALS

Allison, Alexander W, Herbert Barrows, Caesar R Blake, et al, eds. *The Norton Anthology of Poetry* (Third edition). New York, NY: W.W. Norton & Company, 1983.

Ball, Gordon, ed. *Journals: Early Fifties Early Sixties.* New York, NY: HarperCollins Publishers, Inc., 1996.

Bentley, Chantelle, ed. *Poet's Market: 1,800 Places to Publish Your Poetry* (2000 Edition). Cincinnati, OH: Writer's Digest Books, 1999.

Bowker International Serials Database. *Ulrich's International Periodicals Directory* (35th edition). New Providence, NJ: R.R. Bowker, 1996.

Burack, Sylvia K, ed. *The Writer's Handbook* (1999 edition). Boston, MA: The Writer, Inc., 1998.

"Classifieds," *Poets & Writers Magazine* (Sept/Oct 1999): 104–107.

Conarroe, Joel, ed. *Six American Poets: An Anthology.* New York, NY: Vintage Books, 1993.

Cook, Marshall J, "10 Secrets of Getting Published," *Writer's Digest* (Jan 1999): 22–25.

Council of Literary Magazines and Presses. *Directory of Literary Magazines (1999): Complete Information on More Than 600 U.S. and Foreign Magazines That Publish Poetry, Fiction, and Essay.* Wakefield, RI: Asphodel Press / Moyer Bell, 1998.

Curtis, C Michael, "How to Read Rejection: An Editor's Advice," *Poets & Writers Magazine* (Sep/Oct 1999): 50–55.

Dickinson, Emily. *The Complete Poems of Emily Dickinson.* Thomas H. Johnson, ed. Boston, MA: Little, Brown and Company, 1960.

Dickinson, Emily. *Final Harvest: Emily Dickinson's Poems.* Thomas H. Johnson, ed. Boston, MA: Little, Brown and Company, 1961.

Donne, John. "To Mr. T. W.," *A Critical Edition of the Major Works.* John Carey, ed. New York, NY: Oxford University Press, 1992.

Editors of *Writer's Digest.* "100 Best Writers of Our Century," *Writer's Digest* (Nov 1999): 12–25.

Falter-Barns, Suzanne, "Rejection Won't Kill You," *Writer's Digest* (Sep 1999): 6–17.

Finch, Peter. *How to Publish Your Poetry.* London, England: Allison & Busby Ltd, 1998.

Fooling with Words, With Bill Moyers: Highlights of the 1998 Geraldine R. Dodge Poetry Festival in Waterloo Village, New Jersey. Public Broadcasting System (PBS): 9/26/99.

Fulton, Len, ed. *The International Directory of Little Magazines and Small Presses.* Paradise, CA: Dustbooks, 1998.

Giovanni, Nikki. *Racism 101*. New York, NY: William Morrow and Company, Inc., 1994.

Giovanni, Nikki, and Virginia Fowler (illustrator). *The Selected Poems of Nikki Giovanni*. New York, NY: William Morrow and Company, Inc., 1996.

Holman, Amy, "Simultaneous Submissions: Yea or Nay?", *Poets & Writers* (Sept/Oct 1999): 61, 63.

Hunter, Fred, "A Guide to Dealing With Rejection," *The Writer's Handbook*. Sylvia K. Burack, ed. Boston, MA: The Writer, Inc., 1998.

Lathem, Edward Connery, and Lawrence Thompson, eds. *Robert Frost: Poetry and Prose*. New York, NY: Henry Holt & Company, 1984.

Lesonsky, Rieva. *Get Smart!: 365 Tips to Boost Your Entrepreneurial IQ*. Irvine, CA: Entrepreneur Press, 1999.

Literary Market Place: The Directory of the International Book Publishing Industry (Volume 1; 2000 edition). New Providence, NJ: R.R. Bowker, 1999.

"Market News," *The Writer* (Nov 1999): 27–46.

"The Markets," *Writer's Digest* (Oct 1999): 52.

Miller-Louden, Sandra, "Poetry Does Not Equal Success When Writing for Greeting Cards," *Poet's Market 2000*. Chantelle Bentley, ed. Cincinnati, OH: Writer's Digest Books.

Morris Publishing. *Publishing Guide*. Kearney, NE: Morris Publishing, 1999.

Mutchler, John C, ed, compiler. *The American Directory of Writer's Guidelines: A Compilation of Information for Freelancers From More Than 1,300 Magazine Editors and Book Publishers* (Second edition). Clovis, CA: Quill Driver Books/Word Dancer Press, Inc., 1998.

Obstfeld, Raymond, "How to Make Your Writer's Group Better," *Writer's Digest* (Sept 1999): 44–47.

Pinsky, Robert. *The Figured Wheel: New And Collected Poems 1966–1996.* New York, NY: Farrar, Straus, and Giroux, 1996.

Rosenthal, ML. *Poetry and the Common Life.* New York, NY: Oxford University Press, 1974.

Seba, Jaime A, "E-Cards: A New Frontier for Freelancers," *Writer's Digest* (Aug 1999): 49.

"Unclassified," *Writers' Journal* (Sept/Oct 1999): 64–65.

Wordsworth, William. "Preface to the Lyrical Ballads," 1805 Version. *Romantic Period Verse.* Jerome McGann, ed. New York, NY: Oxford University Press, 1994.

"Writers' Journal Market Report," *Writers' Journal* (Sept/Oct 1999): 60–63, 65.

Zbar, Jeffery D, "20 Tips to Better Time Management," *Writer's Digest* (Aug 1999): 27–30.

Zbar, Jeffery D, "Six Keys to Home Office Success," *Writer's Digest* (Jul 1999): 32–34.

Zehl, Valerie, "Crafting Greeting Cards That Sell," *Writer's Digest* (Aug 1999): 47–49.

WEBSITES

http://lcweb.loc.gov/copyright. United States Copyright Office, The Library of Congress.

http://longman.awl.com/kennedy/brooks/biography.html. "Gwendolyn Brooks," Literature Online: Poetry Author Casebooks.

http://members.aol.com/Raven763/index.html. *The Rose & Thorn: A Literary Ezine.*

http://theanimist.netgazer.net.au/. *The Animist.*

http://webdelsol.com. Web Del Sol.

http://whatiscopyright.org. "What Is Copyright Protection?", Rebecca Delgado-Martinez Valette, Esq.

http://wings.buffalo.edu/epc. "EPC," Electronic Poetry Center, SUNY Buffalo.

http://www.brownbooks.com/self.htm. "What is self-publishing?," Brown Books, Milli Brown.

http://www.buybooksontheweb.com. Buy Books on the Web.com.

http://www.factsheet5.com. "FAQs," Factsheet5.Com.

http://www.geocities.com/Athens/Acropolis/7101/poetfest.htm "Welcome to Poetfest," Poetfest Publications, Robert J. Tiess.

http://www.hanksville.org/storytellers/luci/. "Luci Tapahonso," Karen Strom and Luci Tapahonso.

http://www.litline.html. "LitLine: A not-for-profit website for the independent literary community," LitLine.

http://www.litline.org/html/harris2.html. "Independent Presses and the Future of Contemporary American Literature," LitLine, Charles B Harris.

http://www.microtec.net/lamiel. *Pyrowords.*

http://www.novalearn.com. "Markets," Writer Online, Clare Mann and Cindy Mindell-Wong, eds.

 http://www.poetrysoc.com/info/subpoems.htm. "Submitting your poems to magazines: Advice from Peter Forbes, Editor of *Poetry Review*." Peter Forbes.

http://www.poetrysociety.org. Poetry Society of America.

http://www.poets.org/aap/news/apsum981.htm. "Archie," David Lehman.

 http://www.poets.org/index.html. The Academy of American Poetry.

http://www.poets.org/LIT/poet/ckizefst.htm. "Carolyn Kizer," The Academy of American Poets.

http://www.poets.org/lit/POET/jwjohnso.htm. "James Weldon Johnson," The Academy of American Poets.

http://www.poets.org/LIT/poet/tselifst.htm. "T.S. Eliot," The Academy of American Poets.

http://www.poets.org/LIT/poet/wcwilfst.htm. "William Carlos Williams," The Academy of American Poets.

http://www.prairiepoetry.org. *Prairie Poetry*.

http://www.publishersweekly.com/articles/19990426_71095.asp. "Everybook: The Full-Color E-Book," Publishers Weekly, Calvin Reid.

http://www.publishersweekly.com/articles/19990426_71100.asp. "Rocket eBook Adds Functions, Distributions, Titles," Publishers Weekly, Paul Hilts.

http://www.publishersweekly.com/articles/19990524_71198.asp. "Powell's to Sell Rocket eBook Digital Editions," Publishers Weekly, Steven M. Zeitchick.

http://www.publishersweekly.com/articles/19990927_81207.asp. "NetBooks.com Offers E-Books, Print on Demand," *Publishers Weekly*, Diane Patrick.

http://www.pw.org/info1.htm. "How to Publish: A Guide for Finding Your Market," Poets & Writers, Inc.

http://www.pw.org/RPRT10.htm. "Report #10: Cooperative Presses," Poets & Writers, Inc., Amy Holman.

http://www.pw.org/RPRT16.htm. "Report #16: Multiple Submissions," Poets & Writers, Inc., Amy Holman.

http://www.rutledgebooks.com. "Rutledge Books, Inc.: Partners in Publication," Rutledge Books, Inc.

http://www.sfwa.org/Beware/subsidypublishers.htm/. "Subsidy and Vanity Publishers," Science Fiction and Fantasy Writers of America, Inc.

http://www.sfwa.org/Beware/subsidypublishers.html. "Subsidy and Vanity Publishers," Science Fiction and Fantasy Writers of America, Inc.

http://www.tlcprinting.com. TLC Printing & Copying, Inc.

http://www.u-publish.com/search1.htm. "Library—U-publish.com: How any writer can now effectively compete with the giants of the publishing industry," U-Publish.com.

http://www.users.fast.net/~joyerkes/Item2.html. "A Brief Updike Biographical and Literary Chronology," The Centaurian, James Yerkes.

$\mathcal{I}$NDEX

Written by a publisher with over twenty-five years of experience, this book helps you avoid the common pitfalls that foil most writers, and maximize your chance of getting your nonfiction book into publication.

How to Publish Your Nonfiction Book begins by helping you define your book's category, audience, and marketplace so that you know exactly where your book "fits in." Following this, you'll be guided in choosing the best publishing companies for your book, and crafting a winning submissions package. Then the Square One System will tell you exactly how to submit your package so that you optimize success, while minimizing time, cost, and effort. A special section on contracts will turn legal mumbo-jumbo into plain English, allowing you to be a savvy player in the contract game. Most important, this book will help you avoid the errors that so often prevent writers from reaching their goal.

So stop dreaming of publishing success, and achieve it. *How to Publish Your Nonfiction Book* provides a proven system that will guide you in taking your work from manuscript to printed book.

$16.95 • 288 pgs • 7¹/₂ x 9-inch • Paperback • ISBN 0-7570-0000-2

In today's topsy-turvy world of film production, getting a screenplay sold and produced is no easy task. To play the film game, you need to know the rules. *How to Sell Your Screenplay* not only lets you in on the rules, but also lets you in on the secrets of winning the game.

Written by two veteran screenwriters, *How to Sell Your Screenplay* was designed as a complete guide to getting your screenplay seen, read, and sold. The book begins by giving you an insider's understanding of how the business works. It then guides you in putting your script into the proper format so that you can make the best first impression. Later chapters introduce you to the roles of the "players," including agents, lawyers, producers, and more; guide you in preparing a perfect pitch; provide you with the proven Square One System for query submission; and aid you in getting the best contract possible.

Every screenwriter dreams of getting that lucky break. But the pros know that you need more than luck to succeed—you need to make all the right moves.

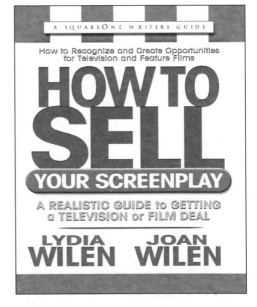

$16.95 • 288 pgs • 7¹/₂ x 9-inch • Paperback • ISBN 0-7570-0002-9

For more information about our books, visit our website at www.squareonepublishers.com.